DAILY ITALIAN

Tobie Puttock

PANNA
UN LITRO E MEZZO

ANALISI BATTERIOLOGICA

eseguita dal Servizio Multizonale di Prevenzione dell'U.S.L. 10/A di Firenze – autorizzato ad effettuare esami completi di acqua minerali con D.M. dell'11 ottobre 1985: Giudizio: L'acqua minerale PANNA, sulla base dei risultati su campioni prelevati alle sorgenti, è da considerarsi batteriologicamente pura.

Firenze, 10 Giugno 1982

L'ANALISTA
Dr. MAURIZIO BIAGINI

IL DIRETTORE
Dr. FRANCO FRANCIOSI

1,5 ℓ   e

8 000815 303206

Vendita autorizzata con Delibera Giunta Reg. Toscana n. 304 dell'1.8.1961, n. 427 del 17.1.1983 e n. 9950 del 3.10.1983

NTE PANNA S.p.A. - FIRENZE
Stabilimento di produzione
Comune di Scarperia (Firenze)

SORGENTE PANNA S.p.A
Stabilimento di produ,
PANNA - Comune di Scarp

DAILY ITALIAN

Tobie Puttock

Foreword by Jamie Oliver

Photography by Mark Chew

Illustrations by Danie Pout

MITCHELL BEAZLEY

tobi

Mark Gonzales 2005 ......

contents

FOREWORD by Jamie Oliver

I could tell you a lot of things about Tobie Puttock, from when he was a slightly less senior chef. Like the things he used to do to me when we were in the kitchen at the River Cafe in London. Since it was an open kitchen, the customers would sometimes hear peculiar noises coming from our direction! Very embarrassing! I could tell you what happened with a carrot and the walk-in fridge at Fifteen, but I won't! I could tell you about his obsession with wearing women's clothes, but I won't! Obviously I wouldn't want to embarrass him, but I'm sure for every story I've got on him he's got twice as many on me, so we'll call a truce and leave it at that. Or maybe I'll save those particular bits for the foreword to his second book!

Now, let's talk sensibly about Tobie and this book. Over my past twelve years as a professional chef, I've met and worked with many, many people from kitchens all round the world – some inspirational, some pretentious, some good, some bad, some egotistical, some crazy, some even dangerous . . .

I guess I'm biased about Tobie because he's my mate, but he's one of the best. I employed him for four years, and without his help (and that of his best mate, wine boy Matt Skinner – you know, that pretty Aussie boy with the curly hair and the slightly camp pout!), Fifteen would never have started in the UK.

So much has been achieved in the past five years: four Fifteen restaurants, hundreds of students trained, and hundreds of thousands of pounds raised through the Fifteen charity to keep giving opportunities to underprivileged kids. And Tobie will continue this work when he opens Fifteen in Melbourne in 2006. For all of this I owe him a lot, but quite frankly, if he wasn't a top boy there's no way I'd be writing this foreword!

The thing with cooking is that recipes are recipes and cooking really is just cooking. But what makes food taste special – and inspires other people to get cooking or try new things – is whether the person cooking it has personality, a smile on their face and a sense of celebration and fun.

Tobie has all these qualities. What I love about him is that not only is he a great cook, but he also loves life along with snowboarding and skateboarding. He's utterly romantic, and he's loyal to his missus and his good friends, and he loves to have a laugh. I believe his passion for life and his pleasantness come out in his cooking – and certainly in this book. And having known him for nearly ten years now, I can't tell you how proud I am that my mate has written such a great book. As you can see from the recipes, words and pictures, it's a wonderful collection of simple, accessible, light, tasty, clean and healthy dishes that modern-day people want to eat. I certainly do!

Some of my favourites are his Tuscan-style Pâté, his Grilled Mussels with Breadcrumbs and Chilli, his lovely Squid Stuffed with Ricotta, Breadcrumbs, Chilli and Marjoram, and his Sausage and Fennel Risotto (looks like one of mine, you little bastard!). And don't forget to try the incredible Veal Cutlets with Fontina alla Mountain Style or the top Pan-roasted Pork Cutlets with Balsamic

'THE BOY HAS WORKED IN GREAT PLACES. HE HAS TRAVELLED AND WORKED IN ITALY A LOT – HE KNOWS WHAT HE'S TALKING ABOUT.'

Vinegar and Thyme. Not to mention the Tuna with Cherry Tomatoes, Vermouth and Basil or the Baked Peaches with Amaretto. All delicious!

Tobie's cooking is not pretentious and he's definitely more interested in flavour and ingredients, and fitting those into normal life, than in building architectural penis-extensions that look pretty on a plate! I've no doubt that the British public will love his recipes and enjoy cooking his food. I can't wait to open Fifteen Melbourne with him and to celebrate Australian cooking and ingredients – headed up by a good-quality Aussie boy.

Loads of love,

Jamie, Jools, Poppy and Daisy

PS: Tobie – my father always said never trust a man who loves cats. You've got two years to lose the cats and bang out some babies, big boy, or else that's us over!

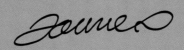

BRUCE SAYS
SHINE ON
YOU CRAZY
DIAMOND

The food,
the book
& me

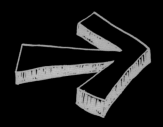

ME FIRST

I don't know what it is about me and Italian food. Fate has constantly led me in that direction, and my own interest and inclination have kept me on the path. I have travelled and worked in Australia, London and Switzerland and, for a year or more, in Italy itself, and I have always found myself in Italian kitchens.

Italian food is everywhere partly because Italians are everywhere – they have migrated to the four corners of the globe and their impact on the places they have settled in has been profound. But it is also about the sheer brilliance of a cuisine that has endured and evolved over the centuries – about its flexibility, healthiness, tastiness, lack of fuss and the sheer love with which it is cooked, served and shared.

My first job was in an Italian kitchen in Melbourne. I had finished school and was looking for a way of earning money to go snowboarding in Europe. My dad, ever practical, told me to get a job washing dishes and sent me around the corner to Caffé e Cucina, which he'd found by looking up the latest *Good Food Guide*.

Restaurateur extraordinaire Maurizio Terzini had opened Caffé e Cucina in 1988. It was a tiny place with a funky but traditional Italian fit-out, waiters in ties and aprons, and authentic Italian cooking. In just three years, it had developed a serious reputation for its food and was at the top of the cool people's register of places to be seen. If I'd known any of this, I'd have thought twice about rocking up with my school report and résumé.

I got a job – food prep, not dishwashing – and somehow I fitted in. The kitchen was tiny, and it was always full of guys shouting in Italian, their noisy rants (usually at or about me) offset by the constant blare of Italian radio. The aromas were amazing – coffee, crayfish, grilling vegetables, garlic being softened in olive oil.

I was there for six years (in between snowboarding excursions), and during that time I discovered what I love about cooking: the joy of good ingredients and the challenge of finding the best way to use them, as well as the sheer fun of working alongside people who are passionate about what they do – those mad, demanding, pirate-like chefs wielding big knives.

I needed to get serious about cooking, so I headed for Italy's north, where it just so happens there are plenty of opportunities for snowboarding as well as cooking. I did a season in a tiny village in the Alps, the most ridiculously scenic place I've ever seen, where I made polenta and salami and lots of dishes with deer. In between shifts I snowboarded to my heart's content. When the snow started to melt, a former colleague from Caffé e Cucina, Daniele Siracuse, found me a job at the Hotel Florence in Bellagio, on the shores of Lake Como.

Lake Como is a scenic wonderland, a vast body of calm water surrounded by fairytale-like mountains. It's meant to be a hangout for celebrities and beautiful people, so I arrived, all keyed up, prepared for endless days of hanging out with gorgeous women, sipping Campari and watching the sun set. It only took me a day or two to realise that the town's population consisted mostly of holidaying retirees, but even if it had been the party capital of Italy, I wouldn't have been up for it.

From the moment I started work, I was pulling double shifts, six days a week. On the seventh day I slept. The head chef was a bloke by the name of Pierre-Paolo Caprioglio. On my first day, he told me he'd speak English to me for a fortnight and after that, Italian. I was in sleep-deprived shock for most of the seven months I was there. When I left it was like escaping a prison. But some months on, I realised how blessed I was to have landed that job: I spoke fluent Italian;

I knew how to make six different types of pasta dough and could roll it with the best of them; I was a sous-chef at twenty-four; and I'd made lifelong friends.

You wouldn't necessarily think of London as the place to experience some of the best Italian food in the world, but that would be because you hadn't heard of the River Cafe. This remarkable restaurant, on the banks of the Thames, has been at or near the top of the list of restaurant greats for many years.

I'd come to England because I wasn't quite ready to go back to Australia after Italy. I approached the River Cafe because I had one of their cookbooks and the food looked pretty amazing. Remarkably, I was given a job. The restaurant was and still is run by Ruth Rogers and Rose Gray, two people I have the most enormous respect for. Their big thing is produce. They source and use the best ingredients available – line-caught fish, diver-caught scallops, free-range livestock (we're talking suckling pigs that roam large forests munching on berries).

On my second day in the restaurant, I heard someone carrying on at the back of the kitchen. I turned around to see this long-haired bloke struggling with something heavy. He was swearing at me – 'fat boy' he called me (I was stick-thin) – trying to get me to give him a hand. Turns out, it was Jamie Oliver. After a few lavish jokes, Jamie and I became well-acquainted. The BBC

had picked him up, and was busy turning him into a superstar. He had just released *The Naked Chef* and was starting to take off.

The River Cafe was fun at times and I learnt a lot. But it was also incredibly competitive. The people there were passionate about food, but they were working for résumés. After ten or so months, it was time to move on. I headed for St Moritz, where I scored a job in a tourist hotel. I cooked 'international' cuisine and clocked off at 2 p.m. each day. For the rest of the time, I snowboarded like a maniac and had big cook-ups with a friend by the name of Michi, a professional snowboarder who wanted to be a chef – in other words, me in reverse.

Back to Melbourne and, once again, an Italian kitchen, this time, a place called Termini. Housed in a disused tram depot in St Kilda, it was a huge success and is still going strong. We established a style based loosely on that of Caffé e Cucina – authentic cuisine, a formal, slightly arrogant service style, crisp white tablecloths, olive oil instead of butter with bread.

It was good for a while, but it wasn't quite enough. Jamie Oliver turned up in Melbourne and told me about a social business – a restaurant – he wanted to set up that would employ young people from seriously disadvantaged backgrounds – particularly those who had been out of work or education for long periods of time. His reasoning was that if you gave them jobs and responsibilities, if you made them part of a team, these kids would eventually build up enough confidence to make careers in the industry. Not only would this business provide a much-needed social service, it was also going to be a top-notch eatery serving ripper Italian food. It was to be called Fifteen, and Jamie was scouting for a head chef.

I didn't need convincing. I cooled my heels for nine months while the restaurant was being fitted out,

then I headed for Europe, once again, with my chef's knives and dual passports. Fifteen was an instant success. People loved it. The A-listers would arrive and mill about with the parole officers who had come to check on their young charges. A TV series was made, which gave the whole enterprise plenty of publicity and added another dimension in terms of sheer intensity. As Jamie had promised, the food was – and still is – brilliant, but it's been Fifteen's social focus that has made it the truly exceptional enterprise that it is.

When it came time for me to return to Australia, Jamie suggested that rather than leave Fifteen behind, I take it with me. Jamie already had plans in place to expand the concept (Fifteen Amsterdam opened in 2004 and Fifteen Cornwall opened in 2006), and Melbourne had always stood out as a likely location. With my decision to return home, the whole thing suddenly seemed doable.

In late 2006, Fifteen Melbourne opened in the heart of the city's central business district. It will have the same philosophy as Fifteen London.

We'll be using the best and freshest produce to make simple but sophisticated Italian food. We'll be bringing in kids who have a history of disadvantage, and training them up from scratch. With any luck, a few of the Melbourne recruits will travel the same path as some of the kids I worked with in London. One, in particular, stands out – a bloke by the name of Ben Arthur.

Ben came from a pretty hardcore background. He was a great big guy with absolutely no confidence. If you left him alone with a task, he'd freak out. We nurtured him through as best we could, but there were times when we thought he wasn't going to make it. Eventually he got a bit of confidence up, a bit of momentum, and he powered on.

He loved Italian food – and was a natural – so the Fifteen Foundation sent him to Tuscany for extra training. About six months later, he's back in England, speaking fluent Italian and making pasta better than guys I know who've been in the business for decades. So there you go – the transformative power of Italian cooking.

THE BOOK + THE FOOD

This may have happened to you. You go to an Italian restaurant in the UK. The waiter shouts 'Ciao bello/bella/signor/signora' as you walk in. You get given a menu written in Italian, which you don't understand. The waiter attempts what is, at best, an imperfect interpretation, because, despite the greeting, he doesn't actually speak Italian.

I've complained about this scenario for so long that it would be completely hypocritical of me to write a book with a whole pile of Italian-language recipe titles. So here you have it – a book of Italian recipes with mostly English titles and no translations.

But this is not the only way I have tried to keep things simple. Many of the recipes here reflect my own tendency, particularly of late, to spend less time in the kitchen preparing food and more time at the shops and markets selecting the right ingredients, based on the logic that the better your produce, the less you have to do to it.

This produce obsession comes from my time in London, where the hunt for the right ingredient has become a bit of a cult. Visit Borough Market on a Saturday and you'll see any celebrity chef worth his or her Michelin star sipping coffee as they trawl the stalls for best-quality quails, goat's curd, duck eggs and stinging nettles.

It goes without saying that Italian food is beautifully suited to this produce-orientated approach. What's better than a bowl of perfectly cooked pasta finished with a hit of your best-quality olive oil and a scatter of parmesan? Or an antipasto made up of a handful of olives, a few slices of prosciutto and a hunk of bread? Like all peasant food, Italian cuisine developed according to the supply and availability of ingredients, and the best Italian dishes are those that privilege the produce – that show it off rather than burying it,

alongside a whole pile of other ingredients, within some elaborate construction.

Getting the best produce in the UK is no longer the tricky and time-consuming business it once was. Whenever I come back after being away, it seems like a whole lot of previously unavailable or hard-to-get items are suddenly everywhere. This applies particularly to organic produce, which is now rife in supermarkets as well as specialist stores. Why use organic ingredients? Ethical arguments can be made about sustainable agriculture and the humane breeding of animals. Then there is the issue of taste and quality. I'm not saying that organic produce will always be better than conventional produce, but most of the time it is.

Having gone on about the virtues of simplicity, I'm now going to warn you that there are recipes in this book that will demand your complete and undivided attention. Think risotto; think rolling and cutting pasta dough; think a slow-cooking piece of meat, roasted or stewed, that needs to be constantly basted and turned. There's a saying that goes: the more you attend to something, the more it will flourish. Cooking is like that. I don't believe in sticking something in the oven – your lamb roast – and pulling it out an hour and a half later. I reckon you've got to keep a watch over your food.

Being an attentive cook will make you a more confident cook. Whenever I've run a cooking class, I've noticed that some of the participants will freak out when I tell them to use a bit less of this or a bit more of the other. They want to know exact amounts. This is completely understandable if you're a novice, but as you get to know a particular recipe, you should be able to start adjusting amounts to suit your own tastes. If you don't like garlic, leave it out; if you're a salt fiend, add a few extra anchovies or capers.

This 'touch and feel' approach will help you get to know both your ingredients and your equipment. All recipe books list exact amounts, times and temperatures, but the truth is these numbers are always a best guess. Baking times will vary depending on your oven; the amount of stock needed for a risotto will depend on the 'thirstiness' of the particular brand of arborio you are using; the cooking time for fresh pasta will be determined by just how fresh the pasta actually is. But don't panic. All these conundrums can be solved by attending to the task at hand – by stirring, tasting, testing, adjusting, basting, prodding and hovering; in short, by devoting yourself to the task.

People with dietary problems know all about the need to be attentive and adaptable when it comes to following recipes. My partner, Georgia, has a common dietary complaint. She loves food and has a brilliant palate, but is limited in what she can eat and often frustrated by the failure of mainstream restaurants and cookbooks to cater to complaints such as hers. So I've decided to here. Thanks to nutritionist Sue Shepherd, each of the recipes in this book contains notes on how to adjust a dish to make it suitable for people with various food intolerances. You can read more in Sue's introduction, 'Good for you', on the following page.

The recipes in this book are all 'cookable' – none are for display purposes only. I don't want you sitting around looking longingly at photographs of complicated dishes that you could never hope to replicate in your own home. I want you in the kitchen, sleeves rolled up, music on, glass of wine in hand, experimenting and inventing, having fun and relaxing, and, most of all, experiencing first-hand the pleasure of good food and the privilege of cooking it for others.

GOOD FOR YOU by Sue Shepherd

(Accredited Practising Dietitian, B App Sc (Health Promotion), MSc Nut & Diet, PhD researcher)

As a dietitian specialising in the treatment of dietary intolerances, I was thrilled when Tobie Puttock asked me to provide information on how to make his wonderful Italian recipes available to people with the following dietary complaints: dairy intolerance, gluten intolerance (coeliac disease), lactose intolerance and irritable bowel syndrome (see opposite for descriptions).

I have provided this information as a series of notes, titled 'Variations for wellbeing', which appear at the end of each recipe. The variations are suggestions for those in need, and do not affect the recipes as written. In other words, there are still many recipes that call for cream, pungent cheeses, wheat-based pastas, onion-rich sauces and other such indulgences.

I met Tobie through his partner, Georgia Katz, who is one of my patients. Georgia loves good food, but as a sufferer of irritable bowel syndrome, she is often thwarted in her attempts to cook and eat interesting meals. This is not because so many ingredients are off-limits, although a few are. It's more that cookbooks and restaurants tend not to cater to the needs of sufferers, even though a reasonably large number of people are affected – 15 per cent of the population in the case of irritable bowel syndrome.

Many people assume that adjusting recipes to make them suitable for sufferers of dietary ailments is a major undertaking, the result of which is bland, unappetising food. But this is not the case, as Tobie's book proves. Most of the variations here involve replacing or reducing a single ingredient, although some of the more complex dishes, such as the pastas, call for more work. The suggested replacement ingredients are readily available in supermarkets, although in one or two cases a trip to the health-food store may be necessary. Most importantly, and without exception, the changes can be made without fear of compromising on the full flavours of the original recipes.

The task of adapting the recipes has been aided by the nature of the cuisine. Italian food is remarkable for its flexibility, but also for its health-giving goodness: it relies on olive oil rather than butter and cream; it uses a large variety of fruit and vegetables, and other fresh natural ingredients that are rich in antioxidants and low in saturated fat; and it strikes a sensible balance between the use of carbohydrates and of animal proteins.

Every effort has been made to ensure the advice contained in 'Variations for wellbeing' is as accurate and up-to-date as possible. If you suspect you have an intolerance, it's a good idea to get specific dietary advice from a dietitian. It's worth noting that food allergies are different from food intolerances, and can involve food triggers other than those listed here.

For those of you who are able to enjoy the following recipes, with or without the variations, buona salute! I am sure you will be as impressed as I have been by the freshness, flexibility, creativity and big-heartedness that Tobie Puttock brings to the art of Italian cooking.

Dairy intolerance

As is evident, this condition requires sufferers to avoid food made from cow's milk products, including milk, yoghurt, cheese, ice cream, cream, milk-based margarine, dairy desserts and custards. Goat's and sheep's milk products make for good alternatives.

Lactose intolerance

Lactose is a sugar that occurs in milk from cows, goats and sheep. Sufferers can usually handle very small amounts of lactose in their diet. Lactose is present in large amounts in milk, ice cream and custard. It is present in moderate amounts in yoghurt and unripened cheeses (such as cottage, ricotta and cream cheeses and quark). Cream contains minimal amounts of lactose. Butter is virtually free of lactose, as are ripened cheeses, such as cheddar, parmesan, mozzarella and gorgonzola.

Gluten intolerance (coeliac disease)

Gluten is the protein component of wheat, rye, barley, triticale and oats. In people with coeliac disease, gluten causes damage to the lining of the small intestine. As a result, the ability to absorb nutrients is decreased, and sufferers can become very unwell. The gluten-free diet permits fruits, vegetables, plain meat, fish, chicken, eggs, legumes and lentils, nuts and seeds, most dairy foods, and butter and oils. Gluten-free grains and starches include rice, corn, soy, potato and tapioca.

Irritable bowel syndrome (IBS)

Symptoms of this common condition include abdominal bloating, wind and cramps. There are many food triggers for IBS and there is no single diet that suits all sufferers. That said, many sufferers find they can control their symptoms, to varying degrees, by reducing their wheat and dairy intake. Some fruits and vegetables are known for making people windy, and high-fat diets often make symptoms worse. The 'Variations for wellbeing' notes for IBS incorporate recipe modifications that minimise the use of these potential food triggers.

NO PLATES BIG TASTES

yum

Dressed cannellini beans

Fried mozzarella with saffron

Broad beans with anchovies

Pickled vegetables

Tuscan-style pâté

Rabbit tuna

Flatbread from Emilia-Romagna

Fried mushrooms with basil and anchovy mayonnaise

Braised shallots in tuna sauce

Marinated sardines

Grilled mussels with breadcrumbs and chilli

Herb frittata with prosciutto and goat's cheese

'IF THERE IS ONE RULE, IT IS THIS : AS ELSEWHERE, USE **THE BEST-QUALITY** INGREDIENTS YOU CAN AFFORD. I WOULD RATHER HAVE A DOZEN PRIZED OLIVES THAN A PLATTER OF SLIGHTLY - LESS - THAN - FRESH OFFERINGS FROM THE PLASTIC TUBS AT THE DELI COUNTER. '

All the dishes in this section are typically what we would call antipasto – small portions of big-tasting food that can be eaten standing up at a party, or from the centre of the table.

Contrary to common belief, antipasto should not be piled onto a big platter, with all the flavours oozing into one another. It's a sad fact that many people's experience of antipasto is exactly this: a sort-of seamless collection of oil-soaked eggplant, rubbery bocconcini, acrid dried tomatoes and oversalted meat. My advice is don't be put off: there's a whole world of antipasto out there, just waiting to be discovered.

On one of my first visits to Italy, some kind friends led me up a winding road to a family-run trattoria, tucked amid the steep hills that encircle Lake Como. The antipasto menu ran to a selection of forty different plates! The first dish we tried was simply four fine slices of best-quality prosciutto; next came a rich polenta, oozing with taleggio cheese; this was followed by cannellini beans, rich with tripe and spicy with chilli . . . Needless to say, after several more dishes and many more glasses of wine, my grasp of the fine detail began to falter.

The point is this: antipasto is what you make it. Put out a handful of olives, a slice or two of prosciutto and some good bread, and you have an antipasto. Alternatively, go to town with grilled mussels in their shells, marinated sardines and braised shallots. Get inventive. Shop around for interesting produce. Go for quality ingredients. Spend more, but buy less, and be amazed at the results.

A point that needs to be made about the recipes that follow is that most, if not all, are completely flexible. They'll all do very nicely as part of a selection of antipasto, but many will double as a light lunch; a stand-alone starter; a side accompaniment for meat, poultry or fish; or a tasty snack eaten at 2 a.m. by the light of the fridge door. For this reason, I haven't specified serve sizes for a number of the recipes in this chapter. However, if you're thinking along the lines of a sit-down starter, most of the recipes here will do four or six serves quiet comfortably.

Dressed cannellini beans

Fresh cannellini beans are fairly difficult to find – you may come across them in parts of Europe, but they are not at all common in the UK. Luckily, the dried version (or tinned) makes an excellent substitute. Cannellini beans need a bit of help in the flavour department – hence the amount and variety of fresh herbs used here. The white-wine vinegar also really helps boost the taste.

300 g (10 oz) dried cannellini beans, soaked overnight
6 cloves garlic, peeled
3 sprigs sage
2 bay leaves
2 tablespoons extra-virgin olive oil
1 teaspoon white-wine vinegar
sea salt
freshly ground black pepper
2 fresh red chillies, finely chopped
10 mint leaves
10 flat-leaf parsley leaves
10 pale celery leaves (from centre of bunch)

Drain the beans. Place them in a large saucepan with plenty of fresh water; add the garlic, sage and bay leaves. Cook for 1½ hours or until the beans are soft to the bite. Place a bit of greaseproof paper over the saucepan to prevent evaporation.

When cooked, drain the beans of most of their water and allow to cool (it's a good idea to keep a bit of water at the bottom of the saucepan to stop the beans getting too dry). When cool, drain thoroughly and transfer to a bowl; add the oil and vinegar, salt and pepper, red chilli, and mint, parsley and celery leaves, and toss well.

Variations for wellbeing
Dairy intolerance, gluten intolerance, lactose intolerance – enjoy as is
IBS – not suitable, although may be tolerated in small serves by some
    sufferers

Fried mozzarella with saffron

Fresh mozzarella is sold in trays of brine at the deli counter of most supermarkets. You'll need the small balls known as bocconcini, which are about 4 cm (1½ in) in diameter.

a pinch of saffron threads
100 g (3½ oz) plain flour
½ quantity Breadcrumbs (see page 190),
    or 1 cup packet breadcrumbs
10 small balls fresh mozzarella cheese
    (sold as bocconcini)
500 ml (18 floz) vegetable oil
finely sliced fresh red and green chilli
    to garnish (optional)

Place the saffron in a bowl and cover with 2 tablespoons of warm water. Allow the saffron to soak for a couple of minutes, then fold in the flour; use a fork to work the mixture to a nice smooth batter.

Lay out a plate of breadcrumbs next to the batter. Roll the mozzarella balls in the batter, then in the breadcrumbs. Heat the oil in a saucepan. Test the oil by dropping in a pinch of flour. If the flour starts to sizzle, the oil is ready. Fry the crumbed mozzarella balls, in batches, until they are golden brown.

Remove with a slotted spoon and drain on kitchen paper. Serve immediately, garnished with chilli (if using).

Variations for wellbeing
Lactose intolerance – enjoy as is
Gluten intolerance, IBS – use maize cornflour instead of plain flour;
    use gluten-free breadcrumbs
Dairy intolerance – not suitable

Fried mozzarella with saffron

Broad beans with anchovies

Broad beans with anchovies

I like to serve these as an antipasto sort of thing, but they are also quite comfortable paired with a nice bit of poached or grilled salmon.

600 g (1¼ lb) fresh broad beans, shelled
5 tablespoons olive oil
1 clove garlic, finely sliced
4 anchovy fillets
a small handful of flat-leaf parsley, roughly chopped
4 tablespoons white-wine vinegar
freshly ground black pepper
a small handful of pale celery leaves
  (from centre of bunch)
finely sliced fresh red chilli to garnish (optional)

Bring a saucepan of salted water to a boil, and have a bowl of cold water to hand. Plunge the beans into boiling water for 30 seconds; drain quickly, then immerse the beans in cold water to stop further cooking. When the beans are cool to the touch, remove their skins using your fingers; discard the skins and put the beans to one side.

Heat the oil in a frying pan over a very low heat and gently sauté the garlic, without colouring it, for about a minute. Add the anchovy fillets and heat for a minute, then add the parsley, vinegar and pepper, and cook for a couple of minutes before removing the pan from the heat.

Add the beans to the pan, and toss until they are well coated with the anchovy sauce. Toss the celery leaves through the beans and garnish with chilli (if using).

Variations for wellbeing
Dairy intolerance, gluten intolerance, lactose intolerance – enjoy as is
IBS – not suitable, although may be tolerated in small serves by some
  sufferers

Pickled vegetables

Pickled vegetables, known as giardiniera in Italy, can be prepared and kept for any time up to a year, provided they are well submerged in vinegar. The vegetables here are typical of the ones I would use, however, there are no strict rules.

Makes 2 × 500 ml (1 pint) jars

1 litre (1 quart) white-wine vinegar
  (have another cup or so available)
a good pinch of salt
3 bay leaves
1 teaspoon peppercorns
4 cloves garlic, peeled
250 g (9 oz) baby carrots or large carrots, sliced
250 g (9 oz) button mushrooms
1 medium cauliflower, separated into florets
1 head of broccoli, separated into florets
extra-virgin olive oil to drizzle

Sterilise 2 × 500 ml (1 pint) jars or the equivalent (see page 194). Pour the vinegar into a saucepan large enough to hold all the ingredients; add the salt, bay leaves, peppercorns and garlic, and bring to a boil. Add the vegetables, then simmer for about 10 minutes. Using a slotted spoon, remove the vegetables from the saucepan, and place in the jars.

Spoon the hot vinegar into the jars – make sure there is enough in each to cover the vegetables; have extra hot vinegar on standby.

Drizzle a little olive oil into each jar and leave uncovered until the vegetables cool. To store, secure the lids tightly and place the jars in a cool, dark place.

Variations for wellbeing
Dairy intolerance, gluten intolerance, IBS, lactose intolerance – enjoy as is

TOIA®

RETR...
PER APPR...
DI OLIVA...
PIATTI A BA...
VERDU...
100%
PROT...

gine di Oliva
a tradizione
Siciliana

PÂTÉ

TUSCAN
STYLE
PÂTÉ

PICKLED
VEGETABLES

pickled
vegies

oil

oli

KNOWN AS

Giardiniera
IN ITALY

Olive Oil

Rabbit Tuna

Dressed Cannellini Beans

Rabbit Tuna
↓

NO TUNA

Pickled Vegetables

PICKLED VEGETABLES

Tuscan-style pâté

This is a straight-up pâté: it's easy to prepare and it comes without all the jelly bits. When making it, you can blend the ingredients to get a nice smooth finish or, for a more rustic texture, chop the livers by hand. Covered with plastic film, this will keep for up to a week in the fridge, and makes a great snack or starter.

400 g (14 oz) free-range chicken livers
2 tablespoons butter
1 onion, finely chopped
2 cloves garlic, finely chopped
1 tablespoon capers
5 anchovy fillets
1 teaspoon rosemary leaves,
  finely chopped
1 glass dry white wine
sea salt
freshly ground black pepper
a small handful of flat-leaf parsley,
  finely chopped
extra-virgin olive oil

Trim the chicken livers of any connective material (gall bladder), then chop the livers into small pieces.

Melt the butter in a saucepan large enough to hold all the ingredients. Add the onion, garlic, capers, anchovies and rosemary, and sauté over a low heat until soft. Add the livers and cook over a medium heat for 15 minutes; splash in the wine and allow it to evaporate.

Remove the pan from the heat. Once the livers are cool, place the mixture onto a chopping board and chop to a paste (if you prefer, this can be done in the food processor). Place the pâté in a bowl; season with salt and pepper, add the parsley and loosen with a little olive oil. Serve with toast.

Variations for wellbeing
Lactose intolerance – enjoy as is
Dairy intolerance – use dairy-free margarine instead of butter
Gluten intolerance – serve with gluten-free bread
IBS – omit onion; serve with gluten-free bread

Rabbit tuna

Before we go any further we should note that this rabbit dish has absolutely no tuna in it; it's so named because its method of preparation – preservation in oil – makes the rabbit flesh as tender as that of tuna. It keeps for at least a couple of weeks, and probably a lot longer. This is a real dish of the land: Italian farmers' wives prepared it for its ease, taste and the fact that it could be stored for ages without spoiling.

The amount of olive oil listed here should be enough for the initial bottling, with a bit left over for topping up the jars as the meat marinates. But you may need even more. The meat effectively 'drinks' the oil, and the exact amount varies depending on the quality of the meat.

The rabbit takes 48 hours to marinate, so don't start preparing this one on the morning of your dinner party. This is delicious as part of a selection of antipasto, or just keep it in your fridge to have as a tasty snack with fresh bread.

Makes 2 × 500 ml (1 pint) jars

**1 young rabbit, jointed and
  body cut into 3 pieces
1 onion, quartered
1 leek, core removed and discarded,
  outer layers roughly chopped
1 large carrot, roughly chopped
1 bunch parsley stalks, chopped
1 sprig of rosemary
1 sprig of thyme
1 bay leaf
2 bunches sage, leaves only
1 tablespoon black peppercorns
15 cloves garlic, peeled
1 litre (1¾ pints) extra-virgin olive oil**

Choose a saucepan large enough to hold the rabbit without crowding. Put the rabbit, onion, leek, carrot, parsley, rosemary, thyme and bay leaf into the saucepan, then fill with cold water to within 3 cm (1¼ in) of the rim. Bring to a boil, then reduce to a gentle simmer; cook until the meat comes away from the bones with ease – about 1½ hours.

While the rabbit is cooking, sterilise 2 × 500 ml (1 pint) open-necked jars (see page 194).

Remove the rabbit from the saucepan to cool; use your fingers to pick the meat from the bones – you're aiming for pieces that are roughly 2 cm (¾ in) in diameter. Put the meat in a clean bowl and let it sit until the excess moisture has evaporated.

Have these ingredients to hand: the rabbit meat, sage leaves, peppercorns and garlic cloves. Divide the ingredients between the two jars. Don't fuss about how everything goes into the jar – you just want to make sure the tastes are fairly evenly distributed. When all the ingredients are in place, douse with olive oil – make sure the meat is fully covered. Allow the rabbit to cool completely, then secure the lids and refrigerate. For best results, leave the meat to marinate for at least 48 hours. Check the jars from time to time, and top up with oil as needed.

Variations for wellbeing
Dairy intolerance, gluten intolerance, lactose intolerance – enjoy as is
IBS – omit onion and leek and use celery instead (2 sticks, finely sliced)

Flatbread from Emilia-Romagna

This wonderfully plain and versatile flatbread from the north of Italy is known as piadina. It is traditionally eaten with cured meats and soft cheeses, but you can fill it with anything that tickles your fancy.

**500 g (1 lb) plain unbleached
  flour, plus extra for dusting
sea salt
3 tablespoons extra-virgin olive oil**

Sieve the flour into a bowl and make a well in the centre. Add the salt and olive oil and about 125 ml (4 fl oz) of warm water. Using your hands, mix the ingredients to form a thick dough.

On a clean surface, knead the dough until it's smooth and elastic. Place it in a lightly oiled bowl, cover with plastic film and put it in the fridge for about 20 minutes (don't clean the bench surface – you'll use it again later).

Divide the dough into egg-sized pieces. Knead the individual pieces until they are smooth. Roll the pieces into circles 3 mm (⅛ in) thick.

Prick the piadine with a fork to prevent them filling with air as they cook. Cook in a super-hot frying pan or a chargrill pan – they only need about a minute on each side.

Variations for wellbeing
Dairy intolerance, lactose intolerance – enjoy as is
Gluten intolerance, IBS – not suitable

serve it as part of an
antipasto, brushed with
olive oil, rosemary + a
squeeze of lemon.

Fried mushrooms with basil and anchovy mayonnaise

This is a delicious way of cooking mushrooms. The eggwhite batter seals the mushrooms as they cook, locking in that wonderful earthy flavour. You'll need medium-to-large mushrooms for this recipe; check with your greengrocer as to what's in season.

10 basil leaves
5 anchovy fillets
½ quantity Mayonnaise (see page 190)
500 g (1 lb) large mushrooms
1 quantity Eggwhite Batter (see page 190)
750 ml (1¼ pints) vegetable oil
sea salt

Use a mortar and pestle to grind the basil and anchovies until they form a smooth paste, or give them a quick whiz in the food processor. Add the paste to the mayonnaise; mix well and set aside.

Have to hand the mushrooms and the eggwhite batter. Heat the vegetable oil in a largish saucepan. Test the oil by dropping in a pinch of flour. If the flour starts to sizzle, the oil is ready to fry. Don't heat the oil much beyond this or the batter will burn before the mushrooms have cooked through. Dip the mushrooms in the batter, then drop into the oil; fry in small batches.

When the mushrooms are golden on all sides, remove from the oil using tongs, and drain on kitchen paper.

Sprinkle with salt, and serve with a dollop of the anchovy and basil mayonnaise.

Variations for wellbeing
Dairy intolerance, lactose intolerance – enjoy as is
Gluten intolerance, IBS – use modified Eggwhite Batter (see page 190)

Braised shallots in tuna sauce

The tuna sauce in this recipe – more accurately, tuna mayonnaise – has been made famous by the Italian dish vitello tonnato (veal with tuna sauce). This recipe employs the simplified version of the sauce: tinned tuna combined with a basic mayonnaise. The more exotic method is to place a piece of fresh tuna in a pan filled with olive oil, then to cook it over a low heat for a long time. The tuna-infused oil is then used in the mayonnaise.

Tuna sauce can accompany a range of dishes – it's great, for example, with finely sliced pork or beef. But I'm a great fan of how it's done here: the shallots provide a lovely sweetness in contrast to the salty, fishy taste of the sauce.

20 small shallots, peeled
olive oil for baking
2 cloves garlic, peeled
4 tablespoons capers
10 anchovy fillets
¾ quantity Mayonnaise (see page 190)
1 × 425 g tin dolphin-friendly tuna,
  drained and flaked
juice of ½ lemon
sea salt
freshly ground black pepper
pale celery leaves (from centre of bunch)
  to garnish

Preheat the oven to 200°C (400°F). Place the shallots on a baking tray and sprinkle with olive oil; cook until brown – about 15–20 minutes.

In the meantime, prepare the tuna sauce. Place the garlic, capers and anchovies in the food processor and blitz to a puree. Turn the processor off. Add the mayonnaise and tuna to the puree, and use the pulse button, cautiously, to combine the ingredients. Taste the sauce, and add lemon juice and salt and pepper as needed.

Remove the shallots from the oven and allow them to cool. Arrange them on a serving dish. Spoon the sauce over the shallots – they should be quite well covered – and scatter with celery leaves.

Variations for wellbeing
Dairy intolerance, gluten intolerance, lactose intolerance – enjoy as is
IBS – omit shallots; pair sauce with veal instead

Marinated sardines

Go easy on yourself and buy cleaned and butterflied (filleted) sardines. Thanks to the preserving power of vinegar this dish should keep for a week or so, if refrigerated.

300 g (10 oz) cleaned and butterflied sardines
plain flour for dusting
vegetable oil for frying
olive oil for frying
500 g (1 lb) white onions, finely sliced
5 peppercorns
2 bay leaves
125 ml (4 fl oz) white-wine vinegar
a small handful of pine nuts
a small handful of raisins
sea salt
freshly ground black pepper

Wash the sardines in cold water, then pat dry with kitchen paper. Set out a plate of flour and lightly dust the sardines, shaking the fillets to remove the excess flour. Heat some vegetable oil in a frying pan – enough so the fillets are half covered but not submerged. Fry the fillets until they are crispy, then drain on kitchen paper.

Wipe out the frying pan, and use it to heat the olive oil. Add the onions, peppercorns and bay leaves, and cook over a low heat without colouring. After about 15 minutes, when the onions are soft, add the vinegar and stir gently. Cook for a further 2 minutes. Add the pine nuts and raisins, then remove the pan from the heat.

Lay the sardines in a shallow dish; cover with the onions and season with salt and pepper. Cover with plastic film and refrigerate for at least 2 days to allow the marinade to penetrate.

Variations for wellbeing
Dairy intolerance, lactose intolerance – enjoy as is
Gluten intolerance – use maize cornflour instead of plain flour
IBS – not suitable

Grilled mussels with breadcrumbs and chilli

This little dish is comfortable as a starter or as finger food at a party. Buy the mussels fresh on the day you intend to prepare them.

1 kg (2 lb) mussels
3 tablespoons olive oil
¼ quantity Breadcrumbs (see page 190)
2 cloves garlic, finely chopped
a handful of flat-leaf parsley, roughly chopped
1 fresh red chilli, finely chopped
extra-virgin olive oil for flavour
sea salt
freshly ground black pepper

Preheat the oven to 180°C (360°F). Rinse the mussels under cold water, and remove their beards – a sharp tug usually does it. If necessary, scrape off any barnacles by using the sharp end of one mussel against the shell of another.

Select a saucepan that has a lid and is large enough to hold the mussels comfortably. Heat the 3 tablespoons of oil over a medium-to-high heat; add the mussels and cover. Once most of the mussels have opened – this will take a couple of minutes – remove the saucepan from the heat, discarding any unopened mussels.

Wait for the mussels to cool, then remove and discard their upper shells. Using a spoon, loosen the flesh from the bottom shell.

Combine the breadcrumbs, garlic, parsley, chilli and a lug of extra-virgin olive oil in a small bowl, then spoon the mixture over the mussels in their half shells. Season with salt and pepper, then place the mussels, side by side, in a baking dish. Brown in the oven for about 5 minutes. Serve immediately.

Variations for wellbeing
Dairy intolerance, lactose intolerance – enjoy as is
Gluten intolerance, IBS – use gluten-free breadcrumbs

Grilled Mussels with Breadcrumbs and Chilli

Herb frittata with prosciutto and goat's cheese

A frittata is a sort of posh Italian omelette, which you can make using almost any combination of ingredients you like. As long as you have eggs, you have a frittata. Personally, I like to make a very thin frittata as I think you get a lighter dish.

Serves 2 as a starter

4 free-range eggs
2 tablespoons cream or milk
1 tablespoon freshly grated parmesan cheese
6 basil leaves, torn
6 mint leaves, torn
a small handful of flat-leaf parsley leaves, torn
sea salt
freshly ground black pepper
1 tablespoon butter
4 thin slices prosciutto
2 tablespoons goat's cheese or cream cheese
extra-virgin olive oil (optional)

Preheat the oven or griller to a low temperature. Break the eggs into a mixing bowl, and add the cream or milk, parmesan, basil, mint and parsley. Season with salt and pepper, then tease the mixture lightly with a fork – just enough to break the yolks.

Melt the butter in a low-sided frying pan over a medium heat. Once the butter has started to brown a little, add the egg mixture and allow it to cook, adjusting the heat as necessary. To brown the top of the frittata, put the pan in the oven for a few minutes, or pop it under the griller.

Lay the prosciutto on the frittata, followed by dollops of the goat's cheese. Finish with pepper and, if you like, a drizzle of your best olive oil. Slice into portions or serve whole on a platter as part of a selection of antipasto.

Variations for wellbeing
Gluten intolerance, IBS, lactose intolerance – enjoy as is
Dairy intolerance – use goat's or sheep's cheese instead of parmesan

EARLY STUFF *sitting up*

Farro (spelt) soup with vegetables

Pumpkin soup

Salmon carpaccio

Cabbage, crostini and fontina soup

Broccolini with mozzarella, cured lemon and anchovies

Mussel and clam soup

Homemade gravlax

Onion soup with fontina and crostini

Squid stuffed with ricotta, breadcrumbs, chilli and marjoram

Raw beef fillet with lemon, parmesan, thyme and extra-virgin olive oil

Bresaola with parmesan, lemon, horseradish and rye bread

Baked sardines with marjoram

Veal crudo (raw) with mushrooms

Pearl barley soup

Lobster carpaccio

'...I WANT TO STRESS **FLEXIBILITY**. IF YOU WANT TO, SAY, SERVE THE SARDINES AS A MAIN MEAL, DOUBLE THE AMOUNT AND GO FOR IT. LIKEWISE WITH THE FLAVOURINGS. IF YOU ARE A CHILLI LOVER, ADD TWICE WHAT I RECOMMEND. IF YOU ARE AVERSE TO GARLIC...LEAVE IT OUT.'

These are the starters you have to sit up at the table to enjoy. A lot of the dishes in this section are wonderfully simple and, if you're a multi-tasker, can be whipped up as you simultaneously baste the roasting duck for the main, add the finishing touches to your cherry tart, and have another gulp of that nice young sauv blanc you've just uncorked.

Many of these recipes have appeared in various guises in loads of books and on menus around the world. What I'm saying here is that I'm not reinventing the wheel by offering a recipe for, say, gravlax or pumpkin soup. What I am doing is sharing my take on a few old favourites, some of which have probably been kicking around for decades, if not centuries, and which have certainly been a part of my repertoire since I first started out in kitchens.

Soups are a big favourite of mine. I'll often skip the rest of the meal and just eat soup for dinner. As a result, many of my soups are big hearty numbers, some inspired by the steaming, almost stew-like broths you get in the European Alps – perfect stomach warmers after a day on the slopes.

The non-soup starters tend to be more summery. I love recipes that use uncooked or cured fish or meat, and there's a few of them here. These kinds of dishes – light, healthy, but absolutely full of flavour – are the perfect complement to a heavier, more 'prepared' main course. Needless to say, when you use fish or meat in this way, you've got to go for absolute best quality.

By now you may have caught on to the fact that I have a bit of a thing about being flexible with ingredients. With these recipes, as elsewhere, experiment. Add more chilli, use less anchovy – it's about your taste, and that of your guests. Here's an example: my dad doesn't like garlic (I can't believe we have the same genes!), so if I'm cooking for him, I tend to leave it out or reduce the amount by, say, half. There's another approach that is also worth a try. Hold your gaze steady and say, 'Garlic! What garlic?' If this doesn't fix the problem, another generous lug of wine probably will.

Farro (spelt) soup with vegetables

Farro is a very fine-grained type of wheat but it puffs up like a rice bubble. In this recipe, it forms the base for a really simple, earthy soup. The trick is to use a nice grassy olive oil when serving – it will add sophistication to this old hippy favourite.

Serves 6 with leftovers for the flask

3 tablespoons olive oil
50 g (2 oz) pancetta (optional), roughly diced
1 medium onion, finely diced
2 sticks celery, diced
3 cloves garlic, finely diced
a small handful of flat-leaf parsley, roughly chopped
1 tablespoon marjoram, roughly chopped
10 basil leaves, torn
1 × 400 g (14 oz) tin peeled and diced roma tomatoes
200 g (7 oz) farro
sea salt
freshly ground black pepper
freshly grated pecorino cheese to serve
extra-virgin olive oil to serve

Heat the 3 tablespoons of oil in a large saucepan over a low heat, then add the pancetta (if using), onion, celery, garlic, parsley, marjoram and basil leaves; sauté gently.

Once the onion starts to soften, add the tomatoes and about 2 litres (3½ pints) of water. Bring to a boil, then add the farro; season with salt and pepper. Simmer, stirring frequently, for about half an hour.

Serve with pecorino cheese and a lug of extra-virgin olive oil.

Variations for wellbeing
Lactose intolerance – enjoy as is
Dairy intolerance – omit pecorino
IBS – omit onion and double amount of celery
Gluten intolerance – not suitable

Pumpkin soup

The Italians do a few versions of pumpkin soup, but the source of inspiration for this one is closer to home: my dad, who has been cooking this old favourite for as long as I can remember. Once I started to have a go at it myself, I cheffed things up a bit by adding cumin and fennel seeds.

Serves 6 with leftovers for the flask

1.25 litres (2 pints) Chicken Stock (see page 194)
  or Vegetable Stock (see page 195)
4 tablespoons olive oil
2 onions, diced
3 sticks celery, diced
2 medium carrots, diced
1 teaspoon fennel seeds
a generous pinch of cumin
1 kg (2 lb) pumpkin, peeled and cut into pieces
sea salt
freshly ground black pepper

Heat the stock in a saucepan. In a separate saucepan – choose a large one – combine the oil, onions, celery, carrots, fennel seeds and cumin. Cook gently over a low heat for about 10 minutes, then add the pumpkin.

Once the pumpkin starts to soften, add the stock and bring to a boil, then reduce the liquid to a simmer. Allow the pumpkin to cook for about half an hour, or until it's super soft.

Remove the saucepan from the heat and blend the soup in a food processor or blender until smooth. Season with salt and pepper, and serve steaming hot.

Variations for wellbeing
Dairy intolerance, gluten intolerance, lactose intolerance – enjoy as is
IBS – omit onions and double amount of celery

Pumpkin Soup

Salmon carpaccio

This wonderful-tasting dish relies on the age-old combination of horseradish and salmon. The other key to the recipe is the use of seasoned thyme as a rub, which works to add extra flavour and an interesting texture.

Serves 4

1 × 500 g (1lb) salmon fillet, skin removed
5 tablespoons olive oil
sea salt
freshly ground black pepper
1 tablespoon thyme leaves
1 knob horseradish, freshly grated
4 tablespoons crème fraîche,
 plus extra for dressing
juice of ½ lemon
a handful of flat-leaf parsley, torn
10 mint leaves
1 fresh red chilli, finely sliced
extra-virgin olive oil for dressing and serving

Rub the salmon with as much of the 5 tablespoons of olive oil as needed. Combine the salt and pepper and thyme in a bowl, then sprinkle over the salmon. Use your hands to pat the mixture firmly onto the fish.

Heat a chargrill pan, barbecue or frying pan, and sear the salmon for about 30 seconds on each side. You want the salmon still very raw but with a little bit of crust. Set aside.

Put the grated horseradish in a bowl with the crème fraîche, a pinch of salt and pepper and the lemon juice. Mix lightly and set aside.

Slice the salmon into 1 cm (½ in) thick pieces, using a very sharp, thin-bladed knife. Arrange the slices on plates; use your fingers to press down on the salmon so that it sits flat on the plate.

Mix the parsley, mint and chilli with a splash of extra-virgin olive oil. Make sure the herbs are well coated with the oil, then scatter over the salmon. Drizzle the salmon with a little crème fraîche and extra-virgin olive oil, and finish with a grind of pepper.

Variations for wellbeing
Gluten intolerance, IBS, lactose intolerance – enjoy as is
Dairy intolerance – use goat's crème fraîche instead of regular crème fraîche

Cabbage, crostini and fontina soup

This big hearty soup borrows a little from Italy and a little from Switzerland, but its true identity derives from the magnificent European Alps, rather than a single native cuisine. Needless to say, this is perfect fuel for the body after a day spent on the slopes battling the elements.

Serves 4

oil for greasing
500 g (1 lb) bread, preferably ciabatta
1 small green cabbage (or, for something
**   different, try Tuscan kale or curly kale)**
50 g (1¾ oz) butter
1 onion, finely sliced
4 cloves garlic, finely sliced
a handful of freshly grated parmesan cheese
100 g (3½ oz) fontina cheese, roughly torn
freshly ground black pepper
1.5 litres (2¾ pints) Chicken Stock (see page 194)
**   or Vegetable Stock (see page 195)**
extra-virgin olive oil to serve

Preheat the oven to 200°C (400°F) and grease a baking tray. To make the crostini (Italian for toast), break the bread into pieces, place on the greased baking tray and toast in the oven until golden. Remove the tray and reduce the oven temperature to 160°C (320°F).

Choose a saucepan large enough to hold the cabbage; fill with salted water and bring to a boil. Remove and discard the tough outer leaves of the cabbage. Rinse the remaining leaves under cold water. Chop roughly, then plunge the leaves into the boiling water for about 5 minutes or until soft. Drain and set aside.

Select an ovenproof and flameproof dish with a lid – a casserole dish is ideal. Melt the butter in the dish over a low heat; add the onion and garlic and sauté until soft, then remove from heat.

The next stage is about arranging the ingredients on top of the cooked onion, so have the following ready to go: crostini, cabbage, parmesan, fontina and pepper. I pretty much bung all the ingredients in, but I do try to make it so that the various tastes are evenly distributed. Pour the stock over the layered cabbage mixture, cover the dish, and cook in the oven for 2 hours. Serve hot and with a generous lug of extra-virgin olive oil.

Variations for wellbeing
Lactose intolerance – enjoy as is
Dairy intolerance – omit fontina and parmesan cheeses;
    use dairy-free margarine instead of butter
Gluten intolerance – make crostini with gluten-free bread
IBS – small serves only; omit onion and add celery (2 sticks,
    finely sliced); make crostini with gluten-free bread

Broccolini with mozzarella, cured lemon and anchovies

This is a lovely option for a starter. Because it's so light and fresh, it's particularly good if you're cooking a meaty main. The recipe uses a quick-curing method for the lemons, which gives you that delicious Middle Eastern preserved-lemon taste after just 20 minutes. Use only fresh mozzarella – the rubbery yellow variety that gets used on pizzas won't cut the mustard here.

Serves 2

1 lemon
1 teaspoon salt
1 teaspoon white sugar
200 g (7 oz) tenderstem broccoli
300 g (10 oz) fresh mozzarella cheese
8 anchovy fillets
2 tablespoons extra-virgin olive oil
10 mint leaves
10 flat-leaf parsley leaves
10 pale celery leaves (from centre of bunch)
freshly ground black pepper
finely sliced fresh red chilli to garnish

Wash the lemon, then slice it as thinly as possible – aim for 3 mm (⅛ in). The thinner the slices, the better the lemon will taste. Lay the sliced lemons, side by side, on a big plate and scatter with salt and sugar. Leave for 20 minutes.

Bring a saucepan of salted water to a boil. Soak the broccoli in cold water for about 10 minutes, then place it in the boiling water and cook for 2 minutes. Drain, then refresh under cold running water to prevent further cooking. Arrange the broccoli on two plates, along with small chunks of torn mozzarella.

Place the anchovy fillets in a bowl with the olive oil; use a fork to mash well. Add the lemons to the anchovies, along with the mint, parsley and celery leaves. Use your fingers to carefully mix the ingredients, then scatter the mixture over the broccoli and

mozzarella; drizzle with the remaining oil from the mixing bowl. Finish with a generous grind of black pepper and a scatter of chilli.

Variations for wellbeing

Gluten intolerance, IBS, lactose intolerance – enjoy as is

Dairy intolerance – use goat's or sheep's cheese instead of mozzarella (not a perfect substitute)

Mussel and clam soup

This is more of a broth than a soup; the liquid is basically there as a means of keeping the seafood nice and moist, although it's fairly tasty in its own right.

Serves 4

500 g (1 lb) mussels
500 g (1 lb) clams
4 tablespoons olive oil
2 cloves garlic, peeled
3 anchovy fillets
1 fresh red chilli, finely sliced (optional)
a handful of flat-leaf parsley, roughly chopped
2 tomatoes, roughly chopped
1 glass dry white wine
250 ml (9 fl oz) Fish Stock (see page 195) or water
freshly ground black pepper

Rinse the mussels and clams under cold water. Remove the beards of the mussels (a sharp tug usually does it) and scrape off any barnacles by using the sharp end of one mussel against the shell of another.

Heat the oil in a deep frying pan; add the garlic, anchovies, chilli (if using) and half the parsley, and sauté over a low heat for a few minutes. Add the tomatoes; cook for a further 3–4 minutes.

Turn the heat to high; add the mussels and clams to the pan and cook for 2 minutes. Pour in the wine and sprinkle with the remaining parsley; cook until the mussels and clams have opened (discard any that don't open). Pour in enough stock or water to keep the pan moist.

Transfer the shellfish to serving bowls; douse with the cooking liquid and season with pepper.

Variations for wellbeing
Dairy intolerance, gluten intolerance, IBS, lactose intolerance – enjoy as is

Homemade gravlax

I love gravlax and it's always a real treat to serve the homemade version. While it takes just 10 minutes to prepare, it needs to marinate for 2 days. After that, it should keep in the fridge for several weeks. When it comes time to slice the fish, you'll need a sharp, thin-bladed knife to do the job. Gravlax goes really well with a bit of pumpernickel or rye bread, a dollop of crème fraîche and a little freshly grated horseradish. Serve as a starter or as a light lunch, with a handful of salad leaves.

Serves 6

1 bunch dill, roughly chopped
2 tablespoons rock or sea salt
1½ tablespoons sugar
1 tablespoon whole peppercorns
400 g (14 oz) salmon fillets

To make the marinade, mix the dill, salt, sugar and peppercorns in a bowl. Lay the salmon in a dish – a ceramic dish is preferable to a metal one – and cover with the marinade. Cover the dish with plastic film and place in the fridge.

After 24 hours, turn the fish over. Using a spoon, scoop the liquid from the bottom of the dish and baste the fish. Re-cover with plastic film, and continue to marinate for another 24 hours. Repeat the process of turning and basting after 12 hours. When the marinating time is up, pat the fish with kitchen paper to remove residual sugar and salt.

Variations for wellbeing
Dairy intolerance, gluten intolerance, IBS, lactose intolerance – enjoy as is

Homemade Gravlax

SAVE TIME BY BUYING
YOUR SARDINES PRE-PREPARED
- MOST FISH MONGERS SELL
SARDINES CLEANED + BUTTERFLIED
(FILLETED) AND READY TO GO

MANGIARE
(eat)

Onion soup with fontina and crostini

One of the trainees I worked with at Fifteen in London, a great bloke by the name of Ben Arthur, brought this recipe back from his work experience in Tuscany. Traditionally, it's made as a cinnamon and onion soup, and is known as carabaccia. I've given it a personal twist by adding the distinctive taste of fontina cheese.

Serves 4

4 tablespoons olive oil
1 kg (2 lb) onions, finely sliced
4 cloves garlic, finely sliced
2 sticks celery, finely sliced
1 bunch flat-leaf parsley, stalks and leaves
separated and finely chopped
2 sticks cinnamon
1.5 litres (2¾ pints) Vegetable Stock
(see page 195)
100 g (3½ oz) fontina cheese
4 slices ciabatta, toasted
extra-virgin olive oil to serve
freshly grated pecorino cheese to serve

Heat the 4 tablespoons of oil in a large saucepan. Add the onions, garlic, celery, parsley stalks and cinnamon; sauté gently over a low heat for half an hour, stirring every few minutes to prevent the ingredients sticking to the base of the pan. After half an hour, the onions should be browned and sticky (caramelised) but not burnt.

In the meantime, heat the stock in a separate saucepan. Once the stock is quite hot, slowly add it to the sautéing vegetables, a ladle at a time, over the course of a half-hour or so. Continue until you have used all the stock.

Slice the fontina into 4 pieces and place on the toasted ciabatta (crostini); place the crostini under the griller until the cheese melts. Add the parsley leaves to the soup, then ladle the soup into 4 bowls.

Distribute the crostini, giving each one a prod so that it sinks into the liquid. Finish with a big splash of extra-virgin olive oil and a sprinkle of pecorino.

Variations for wellbeing
Lactose intolerance – enjoy as is
Dairy intolerance – use goat's or sheep's cheese instead
    of fontina and pecorino
Gluten intolerance – make crostini with gluten-free bread
IBS – not suitable

Squid stuffed with ricotta, breadcrumbs, chilli and marjoram

I love to use smaller squid when serving this as a starter. The plate looks amazing with several little squid rather than a single large one. Have your fishmonger clean the squid for you, and make sure they reserve the tentacles.

Serves 4

**500 g (1 lb) squid bodies (tubes),
   with tentacles
4 tablespoons ricotta
¼ quantity Breadcrumbs (see page 190)
1 tablespoon marjoram, roughly chopped
finely grated zest and juice of 1 lemon
1 clove garlic, finely chopped
1 tablespoon freshly grated parmesan cheese
sea salt
freshly ground black pepper
extra-virgin olive oil for flavour and dressing
olive oil for greasing
2 anchovy fillets, roughly chopped
2 fresh red chillies, finely chopped
1 tablespoon flat-leaf parsley, roughly chopped
a small handful of feathery fennel tops
   or celery leaves**

Bring a saucepan of salted water to a boil. Cook the tentacles for about 10 minutes; drain, then rinse in cold water. Chop roughly, then set aside.

Preheat the oven to 180°C (360°F). In a mixing bowl bring together the ricotta, breadcrumbs, marjoram, lemon zest, garlic, parmesan and chopped tentacles. Season for taste and add a good splash of extra-virgin olive oil.

Use a spoon or piping bag to fill the squid with the ricotta stuffing, then secure the ends with toothpicks.

Place a sheet of greaseproof paper on a baking tray, and smear it with some olive oil – it's easiest if you use your hands to do this. Place the stuffed squid tubes on the baking tray and cook in the oven for 8–12 minutes or until the squid turns white.

In the meantime, get the dressing going. Put the anchovies, chillies and parsley in a bowl large enough to accommodate the squid. Pour in just enough extra-virgin olive oil to make a rough paste. Season with salt and pepper and add a squeeze of lemon juice. Transfer the squid from the baking tray to the bowl; use tongs to rotate the squid to coat it with the mixture.

Arrange the tubes on plates and drizzle with the remaining anchovy dressing. Finish with cracked pepper, another drizzle of extra-virgin olive oil and a scattering of fennel tops or celery leaves.

Variations for wellbeing
Lactose intolerance – enjoy as is
Dairy intolerance – use soft goat's cheese instead of ricotta
Gluten intolerance, IBS – use gluten-free breadcrumbs

WHEN CHOOSING YOUR PIECE OF MEAT FOR THIS ONE

THINK SUSHI

YOU'LL NEED the best-quality BEEF
YOU CAN BUY, OTHERWISE
IT'S NOT WORTH THE EFFORT

Raw beef fillet with lemon, parmesan, thyme and extra-virgin olive oil

I've made this dish in most of the restaurants I have worked in, and have used various methods to ensure the beef can be sliced paper-thin, such as searing the meat first, or freezing it. I've chosen the following method – tenderising the meat with a mallet – because I think it's the simplest and freshest way to do it.

Serves 4

1 × 400 g (14 oz) fillet of best-quality beef, trimmed of fat
4 slices ciabatta
sea salt
freshly ground black pepper
100 g (3½ oz) freshly grated parmesan cheese
1 teaspoon fresh thyme leaves
finely grated zest of 2 lemons
4 tablespoons extra-virgin olive oil
4 lemon wedges

Cut the beef into 4 equal pieces. Flatten the pieces by placing them, one at a time, between 2 pieces of plastic film, then pounding them with a meat mallet.

Keep going until the meat is about 3 mm (just over ⅛ in) thick, at the point where it starts to tear, then arrange on plates.

Toast the ciabatta. Season each piece of beef with salt and pepper, then scatter with parmesan, thyme and lemon zest. Finish with a generous drizzle (1 tablespoon per plate) of extra-virgin olive oil. Serve with toasted ciabatta and lemon wedges. Squeeze on the lemon just as you are about to eat; any sooner and the citric acid will start to cook the flesh, making it turn pale.

Variations for wellbeing
Lactose intolerance – enjoy as is
Dairy intolerance – omit parmesan
Gluten intolerance, IBS – serve with gluten-free bread

Bresaola with parmesan, lemon, horseradish and rye bread

Bresaola is air-dried beef. It comes from the little Italian town of Chiavenna, in the northern region of Lombardy, and is very similar to a Swiss cured meat called bunderfleisch. Because this part of Italy is very close to Switzerland – towns on either side of the border are separated by just a few kilometres – the regional cuisines share many similarities.

The availability of bresaola varies a little. To be sure of finding it, go to where the Italians shop, such as specialist delis and Italian butchers.

Serves 2

300 g (10 oz) bresaola, sliced super fine
1 knob horseradish, freshly grated
finely grated zest of 1 lemon
extra-virgin olive oil to serve
a small handful of pale celery leaves
  (from centre of bunch)
freshly grated parmesan cheese to serve
freshly ground black pepper
2 slices rye bread

Arrange the bresaola on plates and sprinkle with the horseradish and lemon zest. Add a good drizzle of oil, a scatter of celery leaves and a sprinkle of parmesan. Grind a little pepper over the top, and serve with rye bread.

Variations for wellbeing
IBS, lactose intolerance – enjoy as is (some sufferers of IBS
  may not be able to tolerate rye bread)
Dairy intolerance – omit parmesan
Gluten intolerance – serve with gluten-free bread

Baked sardines with marjoram

This dish does fairly well as either a starter or main. I love sardines. They've got a strong fishy taste, and are packed with omega-3s – fish oil – which means they're good for your memory and your joints, and a few other bits and pieces as well.

Serves 4

400 g (14 oz) cleaned and butterflied sardines
olive oil for greasing
sea salt
freshly ground black pepper
1 tablespoon marjoram leaves,
  plus extra to garnish
2 cloves garlic, finely chopped
olive oil for flavour
finely grated zest and juice of 1 lemon
finely sliced fresh red chilli to garnish

Preheat the oven to 220°C (430°F). Rinse the sardines in cold water and pat dry with kitchen paper. Choose a baking dish large enough to hold the sardines comfortably, and grease with a little oil.

Lay the sardines flat, skin side down, in the baking dish. Season generously with salt and pepper, and sprinkle with marjoram. Place the garlic in a bowl with a good splash of olive oil and a squeeze of lemon juice, then pour over the sardines. Bake for 5–8 minutes.

When the sardines are cooked – their flesh should be nice and pale – remove from the oven and arrange on plates. Finish with a scatter of lemon zest, marjoram leaves and chilli.

Variations for wellbeing
Dairy intolerance, gluten intolerance, IBS, lactose intolerance – enjoy as is

Baked Sardines with Marjoram

Veal crudo (raw) with mushrooms

Of all the recipes I came across in Italy this would have to be one of my favourites. There are a few simpler versions around, particularly those where you don't marinate prior to serving (the veal in this recipe marinates for 12 hours), but I reckon this is the tastiest. Use the best veal you can lay your hands on.

The dish needs a mushroom that is quite moist, rather than a dry, woody variety. Have a hunt in fresh-food markets for slippery jacks or fresh porcini. Otherwise, you could go all out and use truffles – a couple of thin shavings will do the job and probably won't break the bank.

Serves 4

1 × 500 g (1 lb) nut of veal
2 cloves garlic, crushed
1 sprig basil
1 sprig rosemary
1 sprig sage
1 bay leaf
sea salt
freshly ground black pepper
finely grated zest and juice of 1 lemon
200 g (7 oz) fresh slippery jack or porcini
  mushrooms, very finely sliced
thyme leaves to garnish
extra-virgin olive oil for dressing

Cut the veal into several pieces. Flatten the pieces by placing them, one at a time, between 2 pieces of plastic film, then pounding them with a meat mallet.

Use a sharp knife to slice the veal further, this time into very small pieces, 1 cm (½ in) wide and 2 cm (¾ in) long, then transfer the meat to a bowl.

Add the garlic, basil, rosemary, sage and bay leaf to the veal, and mix well. Cover the bowl and leave it to sit in the fridge overnight (12 hours) – long enough for the herbs to really flavour the meat.

Take the marinated meat from the fridge and pick off the garlic and herbs. Season with salt and pepper, and add the lemon juice.

Arrange the veal on plates. Scatter with the mushrooms, lemon zest and thyme leaves. Dress with extra-virgin olive oil.

You'll need to serve this dish immediately. If you leave it to sit, the acids in the lemon juice will start to cook the meat and the wonderful raw flavour will be lost.

Variations for wellbeing
Dairy intolerance, gluten intolerance, IBS, lactose intolerance – enjoy as is

Pearl barley soup

You may have to juggle the amount of stock with this one, depending on how thirsty the barley is. This is a good example of a recipe where you need to have a feel for what's going on. Check the soup constantly, and if the barley is starting to go gluggy, add extra liquid as it's needed.

Serves 6

100 g (3½ oz) pearl barley
1.5 litres (2¾ pints) Chicken Stock (see page 194)
    or Vegetable Stock (see page 195), with a bit extra
    on hand
3 tablespoons olive oil
1 large carrot, diced
1 large zucchini (courgette), diced
1 large potato, peeled and diced
1 leek (white part only), diced
3 sticks pale celery (from centre of bunch)
1 large onion, diced
4 cloves garlic, finely sliced
50 g (2 oz) pancetta, roughly chopped
1 bunch flat-leaf parsley, stalks finely sliced
    and leaves roughly chopped
sea salt
freshly ground black pepper
extra-virgin olive oil for flavour
freshly grated parmesan cheese to serve
crusty bread to serve

Place the barley in a sieve and rinse under cold water, then set aside.

Heat the stock over a medium heat. In a separate saucepan, heat the 3 tablespoons of oil and add the carrot, zucchini, potato, leek, celery, onion, garlic, pancetta and parsley stalks (set aside parsley leaves), and gently sauté over a medium heat without colouring.

After about 15 minutes add the stock to the other ingredients and bring to a light simmer. Stir in the barley, then cover the saucepan and simmer for 1 hour, stirring occasionally.

When the barley is soft, season with salt and pepper, and add the parsley leaves and a really good lug of extra-virgin olive oil. Cover again, then allow the soup to rest off the heat for about 15 minutes so that the flavours can become well acquainted. Serve with parmesan cheese and warm crusty bread.

Variations for wellbeing

Lactose intolerance – enjoy as is
Dairy intolerance – omit parmesan
IBS – omit onion and leek and double amount of celery and carrot
Gluten intolerance – not suitable

Lobster carpaccio

This dish calls for some fairly exotic ingredients. See what you can do in terms of hunting and gathering – the finished result is well worth the effort. Yuzu is a Japanese variety of lime, and you can buy yuzu juice in Japanese grocery stores. If you run out of luck, use fresh lime juice instead. The cresses (baby herbs) may be hard to find – have a hunt in the fresh-food markets. If that fails, you can use mature (normal) basil and coriander. Shiso cress is used mostly in Japanese cooking and is available in some Japanese grocery stores. Purple basil can be used instead and failing that, reinvent the dish with a bit of mint. Cherries are used here, but a pomegranate does the job just as well.

Serves 4

2 lobster tails, uncooked
a small handful of shiso cress
a small handful of basil cress
a small handful of coriander cress
sea salt
freshly ground black pepper
extra-virgin olive oil for drizzling
150 g (5 oz) cherries, stoned and quartered
1 tablespoon yuzu lime juice, plus extra for drizzling
1 fresh red chilli, finely chopped

Use strong kitchen scissors to slice through the lobster-tail shells, and remove the meat, being careful not to tear or break it. Remove the intestines (these extend from the lobster's tail to its belly area and are a brownish colour) and any other icky bits.

Cut the lobster meat into very thin slices using a sharp knife, then arrange the meat on plates.

Put the shiso, basil and coriander cresses in a bowl. Season with salt and pepper and drizzle with a little oil.

Place the cherries in a bowl with the yuzu juice and chilli. Toss lightly, then scatter the leaves and cherries over the lobster, and drizzle the remaining dressing. Arrange the dressed cresses over the lobster, and serve immediately.

Variations for wellbeing
Dairy intolerance, gluten intolerance, lactose intolerance – enjoy as is
IBS – reduce cherries by half; do not use pomegranate

SHAPES AND SAUCES

③

Tagliatelle with cherry tomatoes and sardines

Stracci with peas, broad beans, asparagus, herbs and lemons

Polenta gnocchi with marjoram, taleggio and prosciutto

Rigatoni with veal sauce

Sausage and fennel risotto

Spaghetti cooked in a bag with clams, agritti, chilli and chardonnay

Pea, prosciutto and mascarpone risotto

Buckwheat pasta with cabbage, fontina and potato

Corteccia with duck, sultanas and parsley

Squid ink risotto

Slow bolognese sauce

Rotolo of beetroot leaves and ricotta

Farfalle with smoked salmon, vodka and thyme

Potato gnocchi with prosciutto and sage butter

'...THERE I WAS, SITTING IN THE OTHERWISE EMPTY DINING ROOM OF A RESTAURANT WHOSE PLEASURES I HAD LONG ANTICIPATED, CONTEMPLATING A SERVE OF THE MOST **WONDERFUL** RAVIOLI IMAGINABLE. ALL I WANTED, IN THAT MOMENT, WAS TO LEARN HOW TO MAKE PASTA LIKE THAT.'

When I first started cooking, 'pasta' was the dried stuff that came in packets. I became a convert to the fresh version during a visit to Italy. I had arranged an overnight trip to Venice and, while there, was very keen to eat at the famous Harry's Bar. By an absolute fluke, I discovered my hotel was in the same street. By six o'clock on the evening of my arrival, I was sipping wine and chowing down on a plate of knock-out fresh pasta, all the while plotting my future as a master of fresh-pasta making. It was heaven!

Two years later I was living and working in Italy's well-known resort town of Lake Como. Yes, I was making pasta, but in a rather more full-on way than I had imagined. I was pulling six double shifts a week, two of which were spent at a very long table, in a very small room, rolling the pasta by hand.

From this experience I acquired an enormous right arm and the right to make the claim that, with a bit of know-how, making pasta can be easy. You just need to get yourself organised and, as always, use the right kind of ingredients – special pasta flour, high-quality free-range eggs and the freshest possible fillings and flavourings available.

Everyone has a trick or two for cooking pasta. One thing I like to do is undercook the pasta, drain it, then let it sit in the sauce and a little of the cooking water for a couple of minutes. As the pasta finishes cooking, it absorbs the flavour of the sauce, making it that little bit tastier. But my absolute golden rule is the addition of oil just before serving. This breaks down the starch and stops the formation of those terrible sticky, gluggy nests that we've all experienced at one time or another. It also adds loads of flavour, particularly if you go all-out and use a really good grassy extra-virgin olive oil, which, on its own, will transform a simple peasant dish into a culinary experience.

Tagliatelle with cherry tomatoes and sardines

You should be able to make this dish in about 15 minutes. Good-quality dried tagliatelle is available from most supermarkets. Save time by buying your sardines pre-prepared – most fishmongers sell sardines cleaned and butterflied (filleted) and ready to go. What's great about this dish is that the sardines are cooked very gently by residual rather than direct heat. This seems to preserve the different flavours and allows you to add your best extra-virgin olive oil, without fear of ruining it.

Serves 6 as a starter, 4 as a main

4 tablespoons olive oil
1 small onion, finely sliced
3 cloves garlic, finely sliced
1 stick pale celery (from centre of bunch),
  finely sliced
½ bunch flat-leaf parsley, stalks finely sliced
  and leaves roughly chopped
400 g (14 oz) cherry tomatoes or
  8 roma tomatoes
a splash of chardonnay
400 g (14 oz) cleaned and butterflied sardines
extra-virgin olive oil for flavour
500 g (1 lb) dried tagliatelle

Bring a saucepan of salted water to a boil. Meanwhile, heat the 4 tablespoons of olive oil in a frying pan over a low heat, and gently sauté the onion, garlic, celery and parsley stalks (set aside the leaves) until the mixture starts to soften.

Slice the cherry tomatoes in half (or the roma tomatoes into quarters) and, using your fingers, remove and discard the seeds, and place the flesh in the frying pan with the onion.

Cook the tomato mixture over a high heat, stirring continually; after about 3 minutes add the chardonnay. Allow the alcohol to reduce for about 2 minutes, then remove the pan from the heat. Add the

sardines and a really good hit of your best extra-virgin olive oil. Cover the ingredients in the pan with greaseproof paper and leave to sit for about 5 minutes. The heat from the tomatoes and juices will gently cook the sardines.

Cook the tagliatelle until it's al dente. Drain, then add the pasta to the pan with the sardines. Use tongs to carefully coat the pasta with the sauce. Fold in the parsley leaves and add a splash of extra-virgin olive oil; serve immediately.

Variations for wellbeing
Dairy intolerance, lactose intolerance – enjoy as is
Gluten intolerance – use gluten-free pasta
IBS – use gluten-free pasta; omit onion and double amount of celery

Stracci with peas, broad beans, asparagus, herbs and lemon

Stracci means rags – bits and pieces. It describes the dough scraps that are left over from making other kinds of pasta, such as ravioli. The stracci here are made from scratch by cutting shapes from sheets of fresh pasta dough. In honour of the original method, however, I suggest you get creative with the knife and cut whatever shapes take your fancy. Just make sure the bits are about the same size or they won't cook evenly.

Serves 6 as a starter, 4 as a main

1 quantity Basic Pasta Dough (see page 191)
semolina flour for dusting
150 g (5 oz) unsalted butter
3 cloves garlic, chopped
500 g (1 lb) peas, shelled
500 g (1 lb) broad beans, shelled
100 g (3½ oz) asparagus, woody ends discarded,
    cut into 2 cm (¾ in) lengths
finely grated zest and juice of 1 lemon
a handful of mint leaves, about 20, torn
a handful of basil leaves, about 20, torn
60 g (2¼ oz) freshly grated pecorino cheese
extra-virgin olive oil to serve

Divide the dough in half and roll by hand (see page 192). Alternatively, use a pasta machine: feed the dough through the rollers to create long flat sheets; you may have to feed each sheet through a couple of times, gradually decreasing the thickness setting, to get a nice, smooth effect. Place the sheets on a surface that has been dusted with semolina flour. Using a knife, cut the pasta into odd shapes.

Bring a saucepan of salted water to a boil. In a frying pan or saucepan – one large enough to hold all the ingredients – melt the butter, then add the garlic, and sauté for a minute or two without colouring; add the peas and broad beans.

Drop the asparagus into the boiling water and allow it to cook for about 1 minute. Using tongs, remove the asparagus from the water and add it to the pan with the other vegetables, along with the lemon juice and zest. Keep the saucepan of water at a boil. Add a ladleful of the boiling water to the vegetables. Cook the vegetables at a simmer, shaking the pan to blend the water and butter, then remove the pan from the heat.

Drop the pasta into the saucepan of boiling water and cook until al dente – fresh pasta like this should only take a couple of minutes. Drain, then add the pasta to the pan with the vegetables. Toss in the mint and basil leaves, the pecorino and a good lug of extra-virgin olive oil; serve immediately.

Variations for wellbeing
Lactose intolerance – enjoy as is
Dairy intolerance – omit pecorino; use dairy-free margarine instead of butter
Gluten intolerance – use Gluten-free Pasta (see page 192); use maize cornflour
    instead of semolina flour
IBS – not suitable

oil mint

lemon

lemon

broad beans

Polenta gnocchi with marjoram, taleggio and prosciutto

Polenta is a fine-grained product made from corn. It has been around for generations – a cheap and easy staple for farming families. Traditionally, the only flavouring added was salt. But gradually, cooks started introducing ingredients such as butter and various cheeses – taleggio, parmesan, gorgonzola – and, in doing so, turned a rather bland foodstuff into something exotic and highly versatile. The cheese used here for flavour, taleggio, originates from the north of Italy. It has a brie-like texture and a wonderfully pungent aroma.

Serves 6 as a starter, 4 as a main

1 litre (1¾ pints) milk
350 g (12 oz) coarse polenta
olive oil for greasing
sea salt
freshly ground black pepper
150 g (5 oz) butter
3 free-range egg yolks
a handful of freshly grated parmesan cheese
1 tablespoon marjoram leaves
150 g (5 oz) taleggio cheese, broken into small pieces
10 slices prosciutto

Bring the milk to a boil in a large saucepan. Add the polenta, then reduce the heat. Beat with a whisk to stop the polenta going lumpy, then swap to a wooden spoon once the polenta starts to thicken. Keep stirring until the polenta is soft, smooth and thick – about 30 minutes.

Preheat the oven to 200°C (400°F) and lightly grease a rectangular baking dish.

Remove the polenta from the heat and season with salt and pepper. Fold in ⅓ of the butter, along with the egg yolks and parmesan. Pour the polenta onto a clean bench and, using a spatula, spread it out to a thickness of 1 cm (½ in).

Allow the polenta to cool, then use a cookie cutter or a glass to cut disks of about 6 cm (2½ in) in diameter. Arrange the polenta disks on the greased baking tray in overlapping layers.

Sprinkle the marjoram and taleggio over the polenta, followed by the remaining butter, and bake in the oven until the cheese has melted.

Use a spatula to carefully arrange the polenta on plates. Serve with slices of prosciutto and a good grind of pepper.

Variations for wellbeing

Gluten intolerance – enjoy as is

Dairy intolerance – use goat's or sheep's cheese instead of taleggio; use goat's or sheep's milk instead of regular milk; use dairy-free margarine instead of butter

IBS – use low-fat milk and reduce butter by half

Lactose intolerance – use lactose-free milk or soy milk instead of regular milk

Rigatoni with veal sauce

This is a nice hearty pasta dish. Cook the sauce slowly over a gentle heat – this makes the meat really tender and deliciously rich.

Serves 4 as a main

3 tablespoons olive oil
250 g (9 oz) veal, diced
plain (all-purpose) flour for dusting
1 onion, finely diced
2 sticks pale celery (from centre of bunch),
**   finely diced**
3 cloves garlic, finely sliced
2 tablespoons rosemary, roughly chopped
1 glass white wine
1.5 litres (1½ quarts) Chicken Stock (see page 194)
400 g (14 oz) rigatoni pasta
a handful of freshly grated parmesan cheese
a handful of flat-leaf parsley, roughly chopped
extra-virgin olive oil for flavour

Heat the 3 tablespoons of olive oil in a saucepan that is large enough to hold all the ingredients without crowding. Dust the veal with a little flour and brown it in the oil over a medium heat. Remove the veal from the saucepan and set aside.

Add the onion, celery, garlic and rosemary to the saucepan, and gently sauté; stir continually. Once the vegetables are soft, return the meat to the pan; cook on a high heat for a couple of minutes, then splash in the wine.

Let the wine evaporate almost completely. Add some of the stock – just enough to cover the meat; during cooking, add a little more to moisten the pan as needed. It's really important to make sure the meat is well covered with liquid as it cooks. Reduce the heat, cover and bring to a gentle simmer. Once the veal is super tender (about 40 minutes) take the saucepan off the heat.

In the meantime, bring a saucepan of salted water to a boil and add the rigatoni. Cook until al dente, then drain. Add the pasta to the veal sauce.

Return the saucepan with the veal and pasta to a very gentle heat; sprinkle in the parmesan and parsley. Stir the ingredients until the pasta is well coated. Add a generous swig of extra-virgin olive oil, and serve immediately.

Variations for wellbeing

Lactose intolerance – enjoy as is

Dairy intolerance – omit parmesan

Gluten intolerance – use gluten-free pasta; use maize cornflour
   instead of plain flour

IBS – use gluten-free pasta; omit onion and double amount of celery;
   use maize cornflour instead of plain flour

risotto

Sausage and fennel risotto

Do yourself a favour and use nice sausages with this one – your traditional Italian pork sausages are best, but the recipe also works well with lamb. The sharp aniseed flavour of the fennel gives this dish its distinctive taste and helps cut through the fatty sausage taste that would otherwise dominate.

Serves 4 as a main

5 Italian sausages
1 litre (1¾ pints) Chicken Stock (see page 194)
  or Vegetable Stock (see page 195)
2 tablespoons olive oil
1 onion, diced
2 sticks pale celery (from centre of bunch),
  finely diced
1 fresh red chilli, finely diced
1 bulb fennel, tough outer layers
  discarded, finely diced
3 tomatoes
200 g (7 oz) arborio rice
1½ glasses dry white wine
60-80 g (2¼- 2¾ oz) butter
a handful of flat-leaf parsley, finely chopped
a handful of freshly grated parmesan cheese,
  plus extra to serve
sea salt
freshly ground black pepper

Cut the sausages in half, lengthways; remove and discard the skins; remove the meat and set aside. Heat the stock in a saucepan and keep it at a slow simmer.

Put the olive oil in a saucepan that is large enough to hold all the ingredients. Add the onion, celery, chilli and fennel. Sauté over a low heat for about 10 minutes, or until the vegetables have softened but not coloured.

Cut the tomatoes into quarters, and remove and discard the seeds. Add tomatoes to the pan and cook for 5 minutes, or until the flesh starts to soften. Add the sausage meat and the rice, and turn the heat to medium. At this stage it's really important to keep stirring the rice so it doesn't burn – I find a wooden spoon works best.

Once the rice is translucent, add the wine and wait for it to be absorbed. Next, add the stock, a ladleful at a time, as you stir. Do this slowly, allowing each ladleful to be absorbed before adding the next one. Reserve about 125 ml (4 fl oz) of stock for later use.

Once the rice is al dente, remove the saucepan from the heat and add the last 125 ml (4 fl oz) of stock, along with the butter, parsley and parmesan; season with salt and pepper. Cover the saucepan and leave the risotto to rest for a few minutes to absorb any excess liquid. Arrange the risotto on plates, and serve with plenty of parmesan.

Variations for wellbeing
Lactose intolerance – enjoy as is
Dairy intolerance – use goat's or sheep's cheese instead
  of parmesan; use dairy-free margarine instead of butter
Gluten intolerance – use gluten-free sausages
IBS – omit onion; use onion-free sausages

Spaghetti cooked in a bag with clams, agritti, chilli and chardonnay

This is a great example of one of those easy crowd pleasers. Just make sure no one eats the greaseproof bag – I've seen it happen once or twice. The success of this dish lies with the flavour of the spaghetti. Because it's not quite cooked when it goes into the bag, the spaghetti takes on the flavour of the other ingredients – notably, the wine and the juice from the clams. By the time the parcels come out of the oven, the ingredients will have combined beautifully but still have plenty of texture. The recipe uses agritti, which is a type of marsh grass. It is not essential to the dish, but it does complement it – have a hunt around the fresh-food markets.

Serves 2 as a main

200 g (7 oz) clams or pipis
250 g (9 oz) spaghetti
5 tablespoons olive oil
2 cloves garlic, finely sliced
4 anchovy fillets
1 fresh red chilli, finely sliced
a small handful of flat-leaf parsley, roughly chopped
½–1 glass chardonnay
6 plum tomatoes, roughly chopped
1 bunch agritti (if available), roughly chopped
sea salt
freshly ground black pepper
extra-virgin olive oil to serve
feathery fennel tops to garnish

Preheat the oven to 220°C (430°F). Bring a large saucepan of salted water to a boil.

Rinse the clams under cold water and set aside. Cook the pasta in the boiling water for less than the recommended time – get it out just as it's beginning to soften. Drain, rinse under cold water, then toss the pasta in about 2 tablespoons of the olive oil.

Tear off 2 large pieces of greaseproof paper. The idea is to make 2 bags, which, between them, must be large enough to hold all the ingredients. Place each piece of paper in a high-sided bowl (so that the greaseproof lines the sides of the bowl), then distribute the following ingredients between them: spaghetti, clams, garlic, anchovies, chilli, parsley, 3 remaining tablespoons of olive oil, chardonnay, tomatoes, agritti, and salt and pepper.

Bring the 4 corners of each piece of paper together and tie with string – you'll end up with something that looks like a Christmas pudding. Lay the packages, side by side, in a baking dish, and cook in the oven for 10–12 minutes.

I like to serve the spaghetti still in its bag so that when the guests untie the string they get the full force of what is an extraordinary aroma. Serve with a drizzle of extra-virgin olive oil, salt and pepper, and a scatter of fennel tops.

Variations for wellbeing
Dairy intolerance, lactose intolerance – enjoy as is
Gluten intolerance – use gluten-free pasta
IBS – use gluten-free pasta; reduce tomatoes by half

Pea, prosciutto and mascarpone risotto

At the base of most Italian sauces and soups is a fried mix called soffrito. It can contain a variety of ingredients – peppers, herbs – but the basic version is onion, celery, garlic and a few parsley stalks. The ingredients in a soffrito should be cut so finely that they melt away into the sauce or soup. If your knife skills are not quite good enough for this, chop the vegetables as finely as possible, then give the mixture a couple of quick pulses in the food processor. Purists might sneer at this, but I've seen it done in many Italian restaurants.

Serves 2 as a main

500 ml (18 floz) Chicken Stock (see page 194)
  or Vegetable Stock (see page 195)
400 g (14 oz) peas, freshly shelled,
  or 150 g (5 oz) frozen peas
10 mint leaves, torn
sea salt
freshly ground black pepper
2 tablespoons olive oil
1 onion, finely chopped
2 sticks pale celery (from centre of bunch),
  finely chopped
a small handful of parsley stalks, finely sliced
2 cloves garlic, finely chopped
150 g (5 oz) arborio rice
½ glass dry vermouth or dry white wine
2 tablespoons freshly grated parmesan cheese
20 - 40g (¾ - 1 oz) butter
2 slices prosciutto
2 tablespoons mascarpone cheese

Place the stock in a saucepan and bring to a boil. Drop the peas into the stock and cook. When the peas are soft but not overcooked, transfer them to a bowl, using a slotted spoon. Turn down the heat under the stock and keep at a gentle simmer.

Add the mint to the peas, along with a little salt and pepper; use the end of a rolling pin or a can to crush the peas to a rough texture (some will remain whole) or put the peas in the food processor and press the pulse button a couple of times.

Put the olive oil into a large saucepan and add the onion, celery, parsley and garlic to make a soffrito. Gently sauté over a low heat until the ingredients are soft – but not browned – and starting to melt into the oil.

Add the rice – keep the heat low – and stir continuously with a wooden spoon until the rice becomes translucent – about 5–10 minutes should do it.

Add the vermouth (or wine) and allow it to evaporate almost completely before adding the smashed peas and a ladleful of the stock. Keep adding the stock, a ladleful at a time, while stirring (wait for each ladleful to be absorbed before adding the next one); reserve about 125 ml (4 fl oz) of stock for later use.

Once the rice is al dente, remove the saucepan from the heat. Add the last 125 ml (4 fl oz) of stock, followed by the parmesan and butter; stir until the butter has melted. Season with salt and pepper.

Rest the risotto for a few minutes, then arrange on plates. On top of each serve, place a slice of prosciutto and a dollop of mascarpone.

Variations for wellbeing
Gluten intolerance, lactose intolerance – enjoy as is
Dairy intolerance – use goat's or sheep's cheese instead of parmesan; use dairy-free margarine instead of butter; use crème fraîche instead of mascarpone
IBS – omit onion and double amount of celery

OWNED RICE MILL
RRON
sa"Pila Vecchia")
NCE 1650
DELLA SC
VERONA
SEMIFI
NE NANO
CE OF ITALY
S NET 1 kg

GUSTOSO

(tasty)

COOKING WITH GREAT
INGREDIENTS MEANS LESS
TIME IN THE KITCHEN,
WHICH MEANS MORE
TIME SPENT DOING ALL
THOSE OTHER THINGS
YOU LOVE TO DO.'

Buckwheat pasta with cabbage, fontina and potato

This is food without borders – a little bit Italian, a touch of Swiss, a definite Austrian undertone. But at heart, this dish belongs to the European Alps and, accordingly, should only be served when the weather is cold, the days are short and the fire is crackling (a good bottle of red will complete the picture). This recipe uses savoy cabbage, but you can experiment with some close relatives that are popping up in fresh-food markets – such as cavolo nero or curly kale.

Serves 2 as a main

1 quantity Buckwheat Pasta (see page 191)
semolina flour for dusting
200 g (7 oz) potatoes, peeled and sliced
**¼ savoy cabbage, outer leaves discarded,
    roughly chopped**
80 g (2¾ oz) butter
2 cloves garlic, finely chopped
5 sage leaves, finely sliced
olive oil for greasing
sea salt
freshly ground black pepper
100 g (3½ oz) freshly grated parmesan cheese
100 g (3½ oz) fontina cheese, torn

Divide pasta dough in half and roll by hand (see page 192). Alternatively, use a pasta machine: feed the dough through the rollers to create long flat sheets; you may have to feed each sheet through a couple of times, gradually decreasing the thickness setting, to get a nice, smooth effect. Place the sheets on a surface that has been dusted with semolina flour, and cut into tagliatelle-width strips – about 1 cm (½ in) – and then into 5 cm (2 in) lengths.

Choose a saucepan large enough to hold all the ingredients; fill with water and bring to a boil. Add the potatoes and cabbage and cook for about 10 minutes, or until the potatoes start to soften. Add the pasta and cook until al dente. Drain and set aside.

Melt the butter in a frying pan, then add the garlic and sage; cook over a gentle heat for about 5 minutes.

Preheat the griller to medium. Choose an oven dish (ceramic or terracotta) that is low enough to fit beneath the griller, and grease it with a little oil. Place the potatoes, cabbage and pasta in the dish, then pour the sage and butter mixture over the top. Season with salt and pepper, and sprinkle with the parmesan and fontina cheeses. Place the dish under the griller to melt the cheese – a few minutes should do it. Serve immediately.

Variations for wellbeing

Lactose intolerance – enjoy as is

Dairy intolerance – use goat's or sheep's cheese instead of parmesan and fontina; use dairy-free margarine instead of butter

Gluten intolerance – use Gluten-free Pasta (see page 192); use maize cornflour instead of semolina flour

IBS – use gluten-free pasta; use maize cornflour instead of plain flour; reduce cabbage by half

Corteccia with duck, sultanas and parsley

This is a classic sweet and sour dish. The recipe calls for vin santo, which is an amazing sweet wine the Italians drink with biscotti and pastries. The pasta comes from a tiny village in the Italian region of Piedmont, and its name is the Italian word for bark. Not that corteccia looks like bark – it's more of a cigar shape. The name may describe the preparation process, which involves peeling or shaving off bits of dough.

Making corteccia is a time-consuming business. The trick is to get the whole family involved, then, while they're hard at it, you can kick back and tell them you're busy perfecting the sauce. If you don't have time to do the homemade version (or the family won't cooperate), substitute dried pasta – a short pasta will work best, such as trofie or rigatoni.

Serves 6 as a starter, 4 as a main

1 young duck
1 onion, quartered
2 sticks celery, roughly chopped, plus a handful
    of pale leaves (from centre of bunch) to garnish
2 carrots, roughly chopped
a handful of flat-leaf parsley, stalks and leaves
    separated and roughly chopped
2 bay leaves
1 quantity Basic Pasta Dough –
    white or wholemeal (see page 191)
semolina flour for dusting
3 tablespoons olive oil
3 cloves garlic, finely sliced
1 tablespoon rosemary, roughly chopped
2 tablespoons sultanas
1¼ glasses vin santo or other dessert wine
1 × 400 g (14 oz) tin peeled and diced roma
    tomatoes
1 tablespoon white-wine vinegar
extra-virgin olive oil for flavour

Put the duck, onion, celery, carrots, parsley stalks (reserve the leaves) and bay leaves into a saucepan large enough to hold all the ingredients without crowding. Fill with cold water to cover the duck. Bring to a boil, then reduce to a light simmer.

While the duck is cooking, prepare the corteccia. Peel off a little bit of dough, roughly 1 cm (½ in) in diameter, and roll it between the palms of your hands until it looks like a mini cigar. Continue until you have what looks like the right amount for 4–6 serves. (It's worth knowing that fresh pasta won't puff up as much as dried pasta as it cooks.) Store the pasta on a tray with some semolina flour to prevent sticking.

The duck will probably take about 40 minutes to cook. It's done when the flesh comes away from the bones with ease. Take the saucepan off the stove and allow the duck to cool.

Once the duck is cool enough to handle, remove it from the saucepan but reserve the cooking liquid and vegetables. Pull the meat from the duck, discarding the bones and skin. Shred the meat with a knife, then place it in a bowl and set to one side.

Strain the cooking liquid from the duck into a clean saucepan. Bring the liquid to a boil, then reduce to a simmer. Put the cooked vegetables into the food processor and blend until almost pureed.

Rinse and dry the saucepan in which the duck was cooked. Place it over a low heat with the 3 tablespoons of oil, then add the garlic, rosemary, sultanas and half the parsley leaves, stirring constantly.

After about 5 minutes add the pureed vegetables and continue cooking until the excess moisture has evaporated. Add the vin santo and wait for it to evaporate before adding the tomatoes and about ¾ cup of the duck cooking liquid. Let the sauce simmer gently until it has reduced to the point where it's of an equivalent volume to the duck meat. Remove the saucepan from the heat, then add the shredded duck, vinegar and remainder of the parsley leaves.

Rest the sauce for 15 minutes. In the meantime, bring a saucepan of salted water to a boil. Add the corteccia and cook until al dente, then drain. Transfer the corteccia to the duck sauce. Toss well to ensure the ingredients combine. Add a good lug of extra-virgin olive oil and, if you like, a scatter of celery leaves; serve immediately.

Variations for wellbeing

Dairy intolerance, lactose intolerance – enjoy as is

Gluten intolerance – use Gluten-free Pasta (see page 192); use maize cornflour instead of semolina flour

IBS – not suitable

Squid ink risotto

You can get squid ink from most good fishmongers or specialty stores. If, instead of buying squid tubes (as recommended here), you buy a whole squid and clean it yourself, reserve the ink from the sac, which is embedded near the head. As with the Pea, Prosciutto and Mascarpone Risotto (see page 74), a soffrito mix provides a nice tasty base for this dish.

Serves 4

1.25 litres (2 pints) Fish Stock (see page 195)
4 tablespoons olive oil
1 small onion, finely chopped
2 sticks pale celery (from centre of bunch),
   finely chopped, plus pale leaves to garnish
½ bunch flat-leaf parsley stalks, finely chopped,
   plus parsley leaves to garnish
200 g (7 oz) vialone or arborio rice
1½ glasses dry white wine
1 tablespoon squid ink
3 medium squid tubes, thinly sliced –
   about 3 mm (⅛ in)
1 fresh red chilli, finely sliced
4 tablespoons extra-virgin olive oil
sea salt
freshly ground black pepper

Put the stock in a saucepan and heat to a low simmer. In another saucepan, put the 4 tablespoons of olive oil and add the onion, celery and parsley stalks to make a soffrito. Sauté gently for about 15 minutes, so that the soffrito is soft but not coloured.

Add the rice to the soffrito and stir continuously over a low heat until the rice becomes translucent; add the wine and let it evaporate before adding a ladleful of stock. Add the squid ink, then more stock, a ladleful at a time, while stirring (wait for each ladleful to be absorbed before adding the next one); reserve about 125 ml (4 fl oz) stock (keep it hot).

Blanch the squid in remaining 125 ml (4 fl oz) of stock. Remove the squid after 30 seconds, but keep the stock on the stove. Place the squid in a bowl with the chilli and 1 tablespoon of the extra-virgin olive oil, then season with salt and pepper; give the squid a toss to make sure all the pieces are well coated with oil.

When the rice is al dente, remove the saucepan from the heat and add the last bit of stock and the remaining 3 tablespoons of extra-virgin olive oil.

Let the risotto rest for about 3 minutes, then season with salt and pepper and arrange on plates. Scatter with the dressed squid and finish with celery and parsley leaves; serve immediately.

Variations for wellbeing
Dairy intolerance, gluten intolerance, lactose intolerance – enjoy as is
IBS – omit onion and double amount of celery

Slow bolognese sauce

This is a very rich and warming bolognese sauce. It uses a whole piece of meat, rather than mince meat, which gives it a complex, stew-like flavour and wonderfully fulsome texture. The sauce needs to be made in 2 stages. If you have time, cook it at a leisurely pace over a couple of days. The sauce pairs very nicely with fresh pappardelle, which is a flat, wide pasta – wider than tagliatelle – with slightly curled edges. Failing that, go for one of the old faithfuls, spaghetti or tagliatelle.

Serves 4 as a main

Stage 1
600 g (1¼ lb) beef shoulder or other piece
   suitable for stewing, boned
3 onions, roughly chopped
3 carrots, roughly chopped
2 bay leaves
1 bunch celery sticks, roughly chopped

Stage 2
4 tablespoons olive oil
3 cloves garlic, finely sliced
1 onion, finely sliced
2 carrots, finely diced
3 sticks celery, finely chopped
1 tablespoon rosemary, roughly chopped
1 fresh red chilli, halved lengthways
1½ glasses chianti classico
   or other dry red wine
2 × 400 g (14 oz) tins peeled and diced roma
   tomatoes
extra-virgin olive oil for flavour
finely chopped flat-leaf parsley leaves to garnish

Place all ingredients listed under *Stage 1* in a large saucepan; cover with water and bring to a boil. Reduce to a light simmer, and cover the saucepan.

Check the meat every 10 minutes to make sure the water level stays above the meat most of the time. Use tongs to turn the meat every half-hour to ensure it stays moist all over. After a couple of hours the meat should be tender and almost falling apart; if it isn't, keep cooking.

Remove the saucepan from the heat and let the meat cool to room temperature. While this is happening you can get *Stage 2* of the recipe under way.

Put the 4 tablespoons of olive oil in a large saucepan and add the garlic, onion, carrots, celery, rosemary and chilli. Sauté over a gentle heat for about 15 minutes, or until the vegetables are soft but not coloured. Pour in the wine and allow it to evaporate.

In the meantime, transfer the meat from the saucepan to a bowl, and set to one side. Strain the meat's cooking liquid and pour it over the sautéing vegetables; discard *Stage 1*'s boiled vegetables.

Raise the heat under the vegetables, and cook until the liquid has reduced by half. At this stage, add the tomatoes. Once again, reduce the liquid, this time until it's about the same volume as the meat. Remove the saucepan from the heat, and allow the sauce to cool.

Tear the meat into little shreds and add it to the cooling sauce; splash in a good hit of extra-virgin olive oil and garnish with a handful of parsley. Serve immediately with freshly cooked pasta, or refrigerate for later use – it will last 4–5 days.

Variations for wellbeing
Dairy intolerance, lactose intolerance – enjoy as is
Gluten intolerance – serve with gluten-free pasta
IBS – not suitable

Rotolo of beetroot leaves and ricotta

This is an unusual dish, one not often seen in Australia. Basically, it's a big sheet of pasta, lined with a tasty filling, then rolled up in a tea towel and cooked in the oven. The filling is often made with spinach, but I like to use beetroot leaves for their amazing colour, as well as their distinctive taste and texture. The leftover beets can be used to make Beetroot, Horseradish, Marjoram and Crème Fraîche Salad (see page 151). The quality of beetroot leaves does vary, so if you find that what's available is a bit limp, definitely go the spinach route.

Serves 4–6

2 tablespoons olive oil
800 g (1¾ lb) beetroot (or spinach) leaves
350 g (12 oz) fresh ricotta
sea salt
freshly ground black pepper
180 g (6 oz) butter
1½ onions, finely chopped
2 cloves garlic, finely chopped
2 bunches marjoram, 1 bunch chopped and
** 1 bunch leaves removed (stalks discarded)**
semolina flour for dusting
1 quantity Basic Pasta Dough (see page 191)
2–3 tablespoons freshly grated parmesan cheese,
** plus extra to serve**
a good pinch of freshly grated nutmeg
juice of ½ lemon

Preheat the oven to 220°C (430°F). Choose a baking dish with sides at least 10 cm (4 in) high, and grease with a little of the oil. Bring a large saucepan of salted water to a boil. Rinse the beetroot leaves, then plunge into the boiling water for 30 seconds; drain, and cool under running water; chop the leaves roughly and set aside.

Crumble the ricotta into the greased baking dish. Drizzle with olive oil and season with salt and pepper. Bake the ricotta just long enough

for it to start to brown; remove the dish from the oven, but keep the oven on and at the same temperature.

Heat 1 tablespoon of the butter in a frying pan; add the onion and garlic, and gently sauté until soft and translucent. Add the beetroot leaves and the chopped marjoram (set aside leaves from second bunch of marjoram for later); cook over a low-to-medium heat. After about 5 minutes remove the pan from the heat and set aside to cool.

Make sure your bench is nice and dry, then dust it with a little semolina flour. Roll the pasta dough by hand (see page 192). Alternatively, use a pasta machine: feed the dough through the rollers to create long flat sheets; you may have to feed each sheet through a couple of times, gradually decreasing the thickness setting, to get a nice, smooth effect.

You are aiming for a sheet of pasta that measures 40 cm × 40 cm (16 in × 16 in). This size is quite hard to achieve as a single sheet, so it's best to make a number of smaller sheets and join them together using a little water at the seams.

Carefully lift the square of pasta onto a clean, non-fibrous tea towel. In a large bowl, combine the cooled beetroot leaf mixture with the baked ricotta, parmesan and nutmeg; with a fork, mix thoroughly to ensure the ricotta is well scattered through the leaves. Season to taste and set aside. Wipe out the baking dish and frying pan, and set both aside for later use.

Use a spatula to spread the ricotta mix evenly over the pasta, leaving a 10 cm (4 in) strip at the edge farthest away from you. Very carefully, pick up the corners of the tea towel closest to you, then roll the pasta, in the towel, away from you. Make the roll nice and tight. Don't remove the tea towel – this forms the 'wrap' in which the pasta is cooked. Tie some string around the ends, then wind some more string around the middle to help the roll keep its shape as it cooks.

Line the baking dish with another clean tea towel, then place the rotolo on top. Cover with water and bake for about 40 minutes.

When cooked, remove the dish from the oven and, very carefully, transfer the rotolo from the dish to a chopping board.

Place the remaining butter in the frying pan over a high heat; once the butter has melted, add the marjoram leaves. After a couple of minutes the butter will start to brown and the marjoram will become crispy. Remove the pan from the heat and squeeze in some lemon juice to prevent the butter burning.

Untie the tea towel and remove the rotolo. Cut the rotolo into slices and arrange on plates. Drizzle with marjoram butter and scatter with plenty of parmesan.

Variations for wellbeing

Dairy intolerance – use goat's cheese instead of ricotta and parmesan; use dairy-free margarine instead of butter

Gluten intolerance – use maize cornflour instead of plain flour; use gluten-free pasta

IBS – omit onion and add celery (2 sticks, finely chopped); use maize cornflour instead of plain flour; use Gluten-free Pasta (see page 192); reduce butter by half; small serves only

Lactose intolerance – very small serves only

Farfalle with smoked salmon, vodka and thyme

This is a variation of a dish that has been around for many years. It's normally done with cream and sometimes even caviar, but my version steers away from rich ingredients, resulting in something that's fairly light and fresh. I suggest using farfalle pasta, the little bow-tie shapes that you'll find in any supermarket. You can make your own, but the dried version does very well for this recipe.

Variations for wellbeing

Dairy intolerance, lactose intolerance – enjoy as is

Gluten intolerance – use gluten-free pasta

IBS – use gluten-free pasta; omit onion; use vodka not wine

Serves 4 as a starter, 2 as a main

220 g (8 oz) farfalle pasta
2 tablespoons olive oil
60 - 80 g (2 - 2¾ oz) butter
2 medium onions, finely sliced
3 cloves garlic, finely sliced
1 fresh red chilli, finely chopped
1 tablespoon fresh thyme leaves, plus extra to garnish
100 ml (3½ fl oz) vodka or white wine
150 g (5 oz) smoked salmon, roughly sliced
pale celery leaves (from centre of bunch) to garnish

Bring a saucepan of salted water to a boil. Place the farfalle in the boiling water and cook until it's al dente. Drain and set aside.

In the meantime, put the olive oil and butter in a saucepan and heat gently. Add the onions, garlic, chilli and thyme. Sauté until the onions are soft and translucent – about 15 minutes should do it.

Turn up the heat and add the vodka to the onions. Allow the alcohol to burn off for a minute or two. Remove the saucepan from the heat, then add the salmon.

Add the pasta to the salmon sauce, along with the extra thyme leaves; stir well to coat the pasta with the sauce. Serve immediately, garnished with a scattering of celery leaves.

Potato gnocchi with prosciutto and sage butter

After all these years, I've learnt that baking the potatoes on a bed of salt is the ultimate way to go when it comes to making gnocchi. This method draws the moisture from the potato, leaving a concentration of starch that acts as the binding agent for the gnocchi, thereby reducing the need for loads of flour. The result is gnocchi that is super light, the polar opposite of the ping-pong-ball variety served up by so many restaurants. I get quite emotional when I cook this dish – it's just so good.

Serves 6 as a starter, 4 as a main

a good handful of rock salt
500 g (1 lb) potatoes (choose a high-starch
  variety – ask your greengrocer)
2 free-range egg yolks
a handful of freshly grated parmesan cheese,
  plus extra to serve
a pinch of nutmeg
sea salt
150 g (5 oz) plain (all-purpose) flour
6–10 slices prosciutto
200 g (7 oz) butter
2 tablespoons sage leaves
juice of ½ lemon
freshly ground black pepper

Preheat the oven to 220°C (430°F). Spread the rock salt over the base of a large baking dish. Place the potatoes – in their skins – on the salt, and bake for 40–60 minutes or until the insides are really soft (use a skewer to test). Let the potatoes cool a little, then use a knife to remove their skins – this should be quite easy. Mash the warm potatoes in a bowl, then mix in the egg yolks, parmesan, nutmeg and a pinch of sea salt.

Use a little of the flour to dust the surface of the bench. Put the potato dough on the bench and knead well. As you go, add flour until the dough loses its stickiness.

Bring a large saucepan of salted water to a boil.

Divide the potato dough into fist-sized pieces. Take one of the pieces and roll a long sausage-like shape, about 15 cm (6 in) long and 2 cm (¾ in) high. Use a spatula to squash the dough flat so that it forms a rectangle on the surface of the bench. Lay a slice of prosciutto on the dough, and fold the dough over the prosciutto to form a tube. Use a sharp knife to cut the tube into 2 cm (¾ in) cubes of gnocchi. Repeat this process with the remaining dough and prosciutto. If the dough becomes sticky, sprinkle with extra flour.

Choose a frying pan large enough to hold the gnocchi comfortably. Melt the butter in the pan over a high heat, then add the sage. When the butter is golden and the sage has crisped up, squeeze in some lemon juice to stop the butter burning. Remove the pan from the heat.

Plunge the gnocchi into the boiling water. When it floats to the surface, it's done. This could take as little as 10 seconds if the gnocchi is really fresh (just made). Using a slotted spoon, carefully transfer the gnocchi from the water to the frying pan. Return the frying pan to the stove, and cook over a low heat for a minute or two. Shake the pan to stop the gnocchi sticking to the base. This will also make sure the pieces are well coated with the delicious sage butter. Cook until the gnocchi develops a little bit of a crust, then serve nice and hot with plenty of parmesan and a good grind of black pepper.

Variations for wellbeing
Dairy intolerance – use goat's or sheep's cheese instead of parmesan; use dairy-free margarine instead of butter
Gluten intolerance – use maize cornflour instead of plain flour
IBS – use maize cornflour instead of plain flour; reduce butter by half
Lactose intolerance – reduce butter by half or use dairy-free margarine

ITALIAN PEELED TOMATOES

IN TOMATO JUICE

NET WEIGHT 400g   Drained weight 240g

④

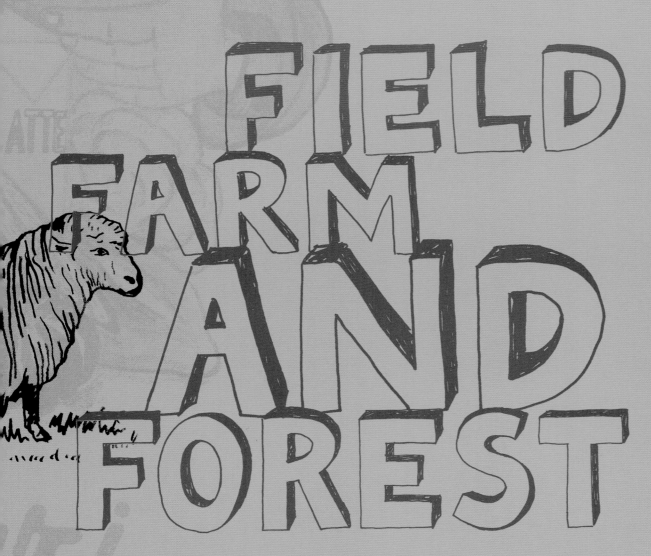

FIELD FARM AND FOREST

Crumbed and fried veal with prosciutto and sage

Pan-roasted pork cutlets with balsamic vinegar and thyme

Roast chicken with fennel seeds, pancetta and capers

Pallard of beef with rocket and lemon

Beef poached in red wine

Christmas or anytime turkey

Braised rabbit with olives and rosemary

Roast duck with amaretti biscuits

Veal cutlets with fontina alla mountain style

Beef fillet rolled in herbs and wrapped in prosciutto

Quails roasted with pancetta and grapes

Slow-braised beef with red wine, orange zest and parsley

'MY MAIN THING ABOUT COOKING — CALL IT A PHILOSOPHY IF YOU LIKE — IS THAT **YOU HAVE TO FEEL YOUR WAY AROUND THE INGREDIENTS** — GET TO KNOW THEM REALLY WELL — AND THIS IS PARTICULARLY THE CASE WHEN IT COMES TO MEAT + POULTRY.'

I'm something of a convert to meat and poultry, having gone through a couple of vegetarian phases. Perhaps because of this, I've become a bit of a stickler for using good-quality meat and poultry, and for being extra vigilant when I prepare meat dishes to avoid wasteful mistakes, such as overcooking.

People always want exact details about cooking and preparing meat and poultry: How much? What sort? How long? I tell them I don't know, exactly. I say it's about the quality of the meat you buy, about the type of oven you have, about how you happen to be feeling on any given day. I say, you have to get to know your meat: prod it, baste it, taste it, adjust the heat, test the juices; in short, treat it with respect.

There's no scientific method that's going to tell you when something is cooked, but there are some useful tips. When cooking poultry, for example, you tip the bird on its side to check the juices that escape – if they run clear, your bird is done.

People think chefs use all kinds of tricks to keep meat moist, but there is only one and it couldn't be simpler: baste, baste and baste some more. As your meat or poultry cooks, the flavoursome liquids drain and evaporate. To make amends, you've got to keep opening the oven or lifting the saucepan lid and spooning those juices – sometimes as often as every few minutes. In short, what comes out must go back in.

Perhaps the best way to make sure your meat and poultry dishes are sensational is to establish a relationship with your butcher that is second only to the one you have with your significant other. If you're going to go to the trouble of cooking these recipes, some of which are reasonably complicated, put the effort into finding an exceptional butcher. Make time to talk to them about what's good on the day; get them to show you a tricky boning technique or two; ask about weight and cooking times. If you can, choose a butcher who sells meat that has been humanely grown and slaughtered, and which is, wherever possible, organic. Yes, it will cost more. But you'll feel good for having done the right thing, and the taste will speak for itself.

Crumbed and fried veal with prosciutto and sage

This is a posh veal schnitzel. Ask your butcher for schnitzel or scaloppine (usually the same thing), and get them to pound the meat so it's super thin.

Serves 2

2 × 200 g (7 oz) veal schnitzel (scaloppine)
sea salt
freshly ground black pepper
8 sage leaves
4 slices prosciutto
3 free-range eggs, lightly beaten
plain flour for dusting
½ quantity Breadcrumbs (see page 190)
5–6 tablespoons olive oil
a handful of rocket (arugula)
juice of ½ lemon

Season the meat with salt and pepper. Press the sage leaves into the veal – 2 per side – then wrap each piece of meat in 2 slices of prosciutto. Push hard on the prosciutto with the palms of your hands to secure it.

Set out the beaten eggs and a plate each of the flour and breadcrumbs. Flour the veal (shake to remove excess), dip it in egg, then coat it in breadcrumbs.

Heat the oil in a frying pan. Fry the veal over a medium-to-high heat until it's golden on both sides. Drain on kitchen paper to remove excess oil. Serve on a bed of rocket, drizzled with a little lemon juice.

Variations for wellbeing
Dairy intolerance, lactose intolerance – enjoy as is
Gluten intolerance, IBS – use maize cornflour instead
  of plain flour; use gluten-free breadcrumbs

Pan-roasted pork cutlets with balsamic vinegar and thyme

The secret of this dish lies in the use of balsamic vinegar: it caramelises as it heats, causing the outside of the pork to become super sweet and sticky. This recipe has been done using pork cutlets, but a loin of pork works just as well.

Serves 2

2 × 200 g (7 oz) pork cutlets
1 tablespoon thyme leaves
sea salt
freshly ground black pepper
1 tablespoon olive oil
2½ tablespoons balsamic vinegar

Using a sharp knife, cut a crisscross pattern into the flesh of the pork. Mix the thyme with a pinch of salt and pepper, then massage the mixture into the grooves created by the incisions.

Heat the olive oil in a frying pan over a medium heat, and cook the pork for 1–3 minutes on each side, or until the flesh is nice and brown.

Splash in the vinegar, making sure to turn the pork over so that both sides get a coating. Once the vinegar has nearly evaporated, remove the pork from the pan and allow it to rest. Add 2 tablespoons of water to the pan, and give it a shake to loosen the vinegar. Arrange the cutlets on plates, and drizzle with a spoonful of the pan juices. Serve with a green salad and Mashed Potatoes alla Tobie (see page 156).

Variations for wellbeing
Dairy intolerance, gluten intolerance, IBS, lactose intolerance – enjoy as is

Pan-roasted Pork Cutlets with
Balsamic Vinegar and Thyme

Roast chicken with fennel seeds, pancetta and capers

This is a good dish for those who like big flavours: there's quite a lot happening, what with the aniseed taste of the fennel and the saltiness of the pancetta and capers. Make sure you baste the chicken during the cooking: the more liquid you reintroduce, the tenderer the meat will be.

Serves 4

1 × 1.5 kg (3¼ lb) free-range chicken
1 teaspoon fennel seeds
1 tablespoon rosemary, finely chopped
2 cloves garlic, finely chopped
sea salt
3 tablespoons olive oil
1 glass white wine
2 tablespoons capers
100 g (3½ oz) pancetta, sliced
1 fresh red chilli, chopped
a handful of sage leaves
a handful of flat-leaf parsley leaves

Preheat the oven to 220°C (430°C). Rinse the chicken under cold water and pat dry with kitchen paper.

Put the fennel seeds, rosemary, garlic and a pinch of salt into a mortar and pestle, and give the ingredients a good bash. Use a tablespoon or so of the olive oil to bind the ingredients as a paste, then rub the paste onto the chicken flesh.

Heat 2 tablespoons of olive oil over a high heat in a large flameproof baking dish.

Put the chicken into the dish and brown on all sides. Add the wine and cook until nearly evaporated. Add the capers, pancetta, chilli, sage and parsley. Place the dish in the oven and cook for 40 minutes, or until the chicken is tender. If the chicken appears to be drying out, add a little water.

This dish goes very nicely with Baked Fennel with Cream, Pancetta and Parmesan (see page 148)

Variations for wellbeing
Dairy intolerance, gluten intolerance, IBS, lactose intolerance – enjoy as is

Pallard of beef with rocket and lemon

This is simplicity at its best. The whole dish takes under 10 minutes to make. It uses a minimal number of ingredients and draws its flavours from their quality, particularly the olive oil, which is used here quite generously.

Serves 2

1 × 400 g (14 oz) fillet of beef
sea salt
freshly ground black pepper
2 tablespoons olive oil
1 tablespoon marjoram leaves
extra-virgin olive oil for flavour
a handful of rocket (arugula) leaves
finely grated zest of 1 lemon
1 fresh red chilli, finely chopped (optional)
2 lemon wedges

Cut the fillet of beef into 2 pieces. Flatten the meat by placing the pieces, one at a time, between 2 squares of plastic film, then pounding them with a meat mallet until they are about 1 cm (½ in) thick. Season the meat with salt and pepper, and moisten both sides with olive oil. Heat a frying pan or fire up the barbecue and cook the meat for about a minute on each side.

Using a mortar and pestle, grind the marjoram with a pinch of salt and pepper, then add extra-virgin olive oil to form a paste.

Combine the rocket, lemon zest and chilli (if using) in a bowl, with more extra-virgin olive oil; toss, and season with salt and pepper.

Arrange on plates. Smear the meat with the marjoram oil, scatter with the dressed leaves and serve with lemon wedges.

Variations for wellbeing
Dairy intolerance, gluten intolerance, IBS, lactose intolerance – enjoy as is

Beef poached in red wine

This recipe calls for a fair lug of wine, so it's important to use something good. I have suggested using an Italian wine, dolcetto d'alba, which is a big fruity red with deep colour. If you can't lay your hands on a bottle, go for an earthy Australian shiraz.

Serves 2

500 ml (18 fl oz) dolcetto d'alba or other good red wine
2 bay leaves
½ bunch thyme
1 teaspoon peppercorns
1 fresh red chilli
2 × 200 g (7 oz) fillet steaks
extra-virgin olive oil to serve

Place the wine, bay leaves, thyme, peppercorns and chilli in a saucepan along with 500 ml (18 fl oz) of water; simmer gently for about 15 minutes to allow the flavours to mingle and mature

Tie string around the beef fillets so they hold their shape as they cook. Immerse the beef in the simmering liquid. Make sure you keep the liquid at a simmer, or the meat will toughen. Cook for about 6 minutes for rare and 8–9 minutes for medium. Remove the beef from the liquid and let it rest for 5 minutes.

Arrange the fillets on plates and drizzle with extra-virgin olive oil and some of the cooking liquid. Serve hot with Mashed Potatoes alla Tobie (see page 156) and Green Vegetables, Braised (see page 190).

Variations for wellbeing
Dairy intolerance, gluten intolerance, IBS, lactose intolerance – enjoy as is

Beef Poached in Red Wine

Christmas or anytime turkey

I made this little number for Christmas lunch once, and it was an instant hit. The recipe calls for a boned turkey; that's because, on Christmas Day, after a few drinks, it's a real pleasure to be able to slice straight through the bird without having to negotiate your way around a pile of bones. If you fancy yourself a bit of a chef, you can bone out the turkey yourself; or follow the path of least resistance and ask your butcher to do it for you.

Serves up to 10

1 large onion, sliced
3 cloves garlic, finely chopped
2 good splashes of olive oil
a good splash of balsamic vinegar
400 g (14 oz) ciabatta, torn into
   bite-sized pieces
100 g (3½ oz) minced pork
1 apple, grated
a small handful of dried apricots,
   roughly chopped
10 dried prunes, soaked in warm water
   to soften, stoned and chopped
a good pinch of nutmeg
a good pinch of cinnamon
80 g (3 oz) prosciutto, chopped
8 sage leaves, finely sliced
1 free-range egg, lightly beaten
a splash of brandy
sea salt
freshly ground black pepper
1 × 4 kg (9 lb) turkey, boned and butterflied
65 g (2¼ oz) fine-grained salt
6 rashers (slices) bacon
4 large potatoes, each chopped into 6 pieces
250 ml (9 fl oz) white wine
250 ml (9 fl oz) Chicken Stock (see page 194)

Preheat the oven to 200°C (400°F). Put the onion, garlic and a splash of olive oil in a frying pan and sauté over a low heat without colouring the vegetables. Once the onion starts to soften, add the balsamic vinegar and allow it to almost evaporate before taking the pan off the heat.

To make the stuffing, place the onion and balsamic mixture in a bowl, along with the torn bread, minced pork, apple, apricots, prunes, nutmeg, cinnamon, prosciutto, sage, egg and brandy. Give it a good mix and season with salt and pepper.

Lay your boned turkey out on a clean bench or a big chopping board. Mould the stuffing into a cylinder shape and place it in the middle of the bird. Bring the sides of the bird together around the stuffing, so that the bird resembles its original shape. Secure with string and rub the flesh with fine-grained salt – this helps make the skin nice and crispy. Finally, drape the bacon rashers over the bird.

Splash some olive oil into a large baking dish and scatter the potatoes around the base. Place the turkey on the potatoes, pour in the white wine and stock, and put the tray in the oven. The potatoes serve as a bed on which to rest the turkey – they won't be suitable for eating.

Cook for 3 hours. Baste the bird as often as possible with the juices from the tray. If you find the skin has browned too quickly, cover it with foil to prevent it burning. Remove the bacon after about 1 hour.

Remove the turkey from the oven and allow it to stand for 10 minutes. Slice using a serrated knife. Serve immediately with a Salsa Dragoncella (see page 193) or Salsa Verde (see page 194), or just good old-fashioned gravy, as well as any manner of roast veg.

Variations for wellbeing
Dairy intolerance, lactose intolerance – enjoy as is
Gluten intolerance – use gluten-free bread
IBS – not suitable

Braised rabbit with olives and rosemary

Rabbits can be found cleaned and gutted at your local butcher. Most butchers will be happy to cut up the rabbit to your specifications – just ask nicely. Wherever possible, use wild rabbit as opposed to farmed rabbit. You can also use hare in this recipe – the meat is a little richer.

Serves 4

**1 × 1.5 kg (3¼ lb) rabbit, jointed and
body cut into 3 pieces
4 tablespoons olive oil
plain flour for dusting
2 cloves garlic, sliced
1 onion, diced
2 pale sticks celery (from centre of bunch), diced
a handful of good-quality black olives, stoned
10 sage leaves, roughly chopped
2 tablespoons rosemary leaves
1 glass dry white wine
1 × 400 g (14 oz) tin peeled and diced roma tomatoes
500 ml (18 fl oz) Chicken Stock (see page 194)
extra-virgin olive oil for drizzling
sea salt
freshly ground black pepper**

Rinse the rabbit pieces under cold running water and pat dry with kitchen paper.

Choose a heavy-based saucepan with a lid. Place over a medium heat with the 4 tablespoons of olive oil. Dust the rabbit pieces in a little flour, and add to the saucepan, browning gently on all sides. Remove the rabbit and set aside.

In the same saucepan, sauté the garlic, onion, celery, olives, sage and rosemary until soft. Return the rabbit to the pan and cook for a couple of minutes, then add the wine.

Allow the wine to evaporate a little, then add the tomatoes and a ladleful of stock; reduce to a light simmer and cover. Cook for about 1½ hours, or until the rabbit is tender. Check frequently – if the saucepan starts to look dry, add more stock.

Drizzle with a little extra-virgin olive oil and season well with salt and pepper. Serve with Polenta (see page 193) or Cabbage with Garlic and Anchovies (see page 152).

Variations for wellbeing
Dairy intolerance, lactose intolerance – enjoy as is
Gluten intolerance – use maize cornflour instead of plain flour
IBS – omit onion; use maize cornflour instead of plain flour;
   reduce tomatoes by half

Roast duck with amaretti biscuits

Boning a duck is a fiddly thing to do if you're a novice. Ask your butcher to do it for you – if you're serious about cooking, you might want to watch their technique. It's very satisfying being able to do these things for yourself, once you've got some confidence up. This recipe can be made using an unboned bird – just allow a little extra cooking time.

The key to this dish is the use of amaretti biscuits: their sweet, nutty flavour really permeates the duck flesh. As with all roasting, the juices tend to leak down into the base of the tray, which is why basting is so important – it reintroduces the flavoursome liquids to the meat.

Serves 4

olive oil for greasing
1 × 2 kg (4 lb) duck, boned and butterflied
100 g (3½ oz) minced pork
100 g (3½ oz) free-range chicken livers,
  roughly chopped
a handful of flat-leaf parsley,
  roughly chopped
5 amaretti biscuits, crushed
½ quantity Breadcrumbs (see page 190)
1 free-range egg, lightly beaten
2 tablespoons freshly grated parmesan cheese
2 tablespoons rosemary, finely chopped
2 tablespoons extra-virgin olive oil
sea salt
freshly ground black pepper
1 tablespoon fine-grained salt
250 ml (9 fl oz) red wine

Preheat the oven to 200°C (400°F) and grease a baking dish with olive oil. Rinse the duck under cold water and pat dry with kitchen paper.

In a mixing bowl, combine the pork, livers, parsley, biscuits, breadcrumbs, egg, parmesan, rosemary and extra-virgin olive oil, and mix well. Season with salt and pepper.

Lay the duck flat (skin-side down) on a chopping board and place the stuffing in the middle of the bird. Bring the sides together around the stuffing so the bird resembles its original shape; secure by binding the duck with string.

Place the duck in the baking dish, then rub its skin with the fine-grained salt. Cook in the oven for about 1½ hours, basting occasionally with red wine and pan juices.

Remove the duck from the oven. Use a serrated knife to carve slices about 1 cm (½ in) thick. Serve nice and hot alongside Roasted Potatoes with Milk, Rosemary and Garlic (see page 156) and Rocket, Fennel and Blood Orange Salad (see page 142).

Variations for wellbeing
Lactose intolerance – enjoy as is
Dairy intolerance – omit parmesan
Gluten intolerance – ensure amaretti biscuits are gluten-free; use gluten-free breadcrumbs
IBS – use gluten-free breadcrumbs

Veal cutlets with fontina alla mountain style

This dish can be done in genuine St Moritz style, using amazingly delicious fontina cheese and homemade breadcrumbs, or it can be done on the run – in about 10 minutes – with packet breadcrumbs and whatever cheese you happen to have to hand. The method is exactly the same, the choice is yours.

Serves 2

**500 g (1 lb) veal cutlets (size of available
  cutlets will vary)
100 g (3½ oz) fontina cheese, thinly sliced
sea salt
freshly ground black pepper
plain (all-purpose) flour for dusting
1 free-range egg, beaten
½ quantity Breadcrumbs (see page 190)
1 tablespoon thyme leaves
100 g (3½ oz) butter**

Remove any sinew from the veal with a sharp knife. Create a little pocket in each of the cutlets by slicing horizontally into the meat, towards the bone.

Stuff the fontina into the veal pockets, and add a little salt and pepper. Use your hands to press down on the meat to make sure the cheese is secure.

Have to hand the ingredients you'll need to crumb the cutlets: the beaten egg (in a bowl large enough to accommodate the cutlets) and a plate each of the flour and breadcrumbs. Season the breadcrumbs with thyme. Flour the cutlets (shake to remove excess), dip them in egg, then coat them in breadcrumbs; use your hands to press the crumbs into the meat.

Heat ¾ of the butter over a medium-to-high flame in a heavy-based frying pan. Once the butter is fully melted, reduce the heat a little and add the cutlets. Fry until they are golden brown on one side,

then flip. Add the remaining butter. If you find the pan is getting dry, resort to plan B: a dash of olive oil. Serve this dish with Potato Rosti (see page 152) and Green Vegetables, Braised (see page 190).

Variations for wellbeing

Dairy intolerance – use goat's or sheep's cheese instead of fontina (although not a perfect substitute); use dairy-free margarine instead of butter

Gluten intolerance, IBS – use maize cornflour instead of plain flour; use gluten-free breadcrumbs; reduce butter by half

Lactose intolerance – reduce butter by half

Beef fillet rolled in herbs and wrapped in prosciutto

This is a wonderfully tasty beef dish, which relies on the flavour of a variety of fresh herbs along with the distinctive, salt-cured taste of prosciutto. The fillet is butterflied and scored, which ensures the various flavours really permeate the flesh. The method also works well with firm, white-fish fillets and pork fillets.

Serves 4

4 tablespoons olive oil
1 × 800 g (1¾ lb) fillet of beef
4 cloves garlic, finely chopped
finely grated zest of 1 lemon
1 tablespoon marjoram leaves
a handful of flat-leaf parsley, roughly chopped
20 mint leaves, roughly chopped
1 tablespoon capers, rinsed and roughly chopped
1 tablespoon extra-virgin olive oil
12 slices prosciutto
sea salt
freshly ground black pepper

Preheat the oven to 200°C (400°F) and grease a baking dish using 1 tablespoon of the olive oil.

Use a sharp knife to remove any sinew from the beef fillet, then butterfly the fillet by slicing it lengthways, but not all the way through. If the fillet is suitable (i.e. thick enough), make a second cut, so you end up with 3 equal-sized flaps of meat.

Use the palms of your hands to press down on the flaps of meat to make them as flat as possible. Using a knife, make a series of crisscross incisions about 1 cm (½ in) deep; this will allow the flavours of the herbs to seep into the meat.

Combine the garlic, lemon zest, marjoram, parsley, mint and capers in a bowl, then drizzle with enough extra-virgin olive oil to bind the ingredients as a rough paste.

Lay the prosciutto slices in 2 rows, side by side, to make a big square. Place the butterflied beef fillet on the prosciutto slices.

Smear the herb mixture over the crisscrossed incisions in the beef, and season well with salt and pepper.

Roll the fillet within the prosciutto, so that it is back to something resembling its original shape; secure the roll with string.

Heat the remaining 3 tablespoons of olive oil in a frying pan over a medium-to-high heat; seal the beef on all sides. Once the prosciutto is brown, transfer the beef to the greased baking dish and cook in the oven for about 30 minutes.

Let the meat rest for at least 10 minutes before slicing. Serve with Salsa Verde (see page 194) and roast veg.

Variations for wellbeing
Dairy intolerance, gluten intolerance, IBS, lactose intolerance – enjoy as is

Quails roasted with pancetta and grapes

Quails, once a rare delicacy, are everywhere these days – check their availability with your butcher a couple of days ahead of preparing the dish. This is one of those poultry dishes where the combination of sweet and salty flavours works a treat, while the addition of a good lug of wine kicks in with a nice rich fruity undertone.

Serves 2–4

4 quails
1 small bunch thyme
4 cloves garlic, peeled
sea salt
freshly ground black pepper
8 slices pancetta, or 4 slices prosciutto
3 tablespoons olive oil
1 small onion, finely diced
2 sticks celery, finely diced
2 bay leaves
2 juniper berries
1 glass dry white wine
2 handfuls of red grapes
250 ml (9 fl oz) Chicken Stock (see page 194)
   or Vegetable Stock (see page 195)

Preheat the oven to 220°C (430°F). Rinse the quails under cold water and pat dry with kitchen paper.

Stuff the cavity of each quail with a few sprigs of thyme and a clove of garlic, and season with salt and pepper. Wrap each bird in 2 pieces of pancetta (or 1 piece prosciutto), and secure with string.

Drizzle the oil into a flameproof and ovenproof dish, and place on the stove over a medium heat. Add the quails and brown on all sides.

Add the onion, celery, bay leaves and juniper berries to the pan. Continue to cook for about 2 minutes before transferring the dish to the oven.

After about 10 minutes, pour the wine over the quails; cook for another couple of minutes, then add the grapes. Every few minutes, baste the quails with the juices from the bottom of the dish. If the pan starts to dry out, add some stock. After 20 minutes, remove the quails from the oven.

Arrange the quails on plates and spoon the pan juices and grapes over the top. Serve with Green Vegetables, Braised (see page 190) for a nice counterbalance to the rich flavours of the dish.

Variations for wellbeing
Dairy intolerance, gluten intolerance, lactose intolerance – enjoy as is
IBS – omit onion; reduce grapes by half

Slow-braised beef with red wine, orange zest and parsley

This is real comfort food, best eaten in the depths of winter. I always pair it with a big lob of oozy polenta. And because I can't resist double serves, I always have to take a bit of a nap on the floor afterwards.

Serves 4

**1 kg (2 lb) beef, sirloin or rump,
  cut into 3 cm (1¼ in) cubes**
plain flour for dusting
6 tablespoons olive oil
2 cloves garlic, finely chopped
1 tablespoon finely chopped rosemary
1 fresh red chilli
2 bay leaves
**½ bunch flat-leaf parsley, stalks and leaves
  separated and roughly chopped**
10 sage leaves
2 onions, roughly chopped
3 sticks celery, roughly chopped
3 carrots, roughly chopped
250 ml (9 fl oz) red wine
500 ml (18 fl oz) Beef Stock (see page 194) or water
**1 × 400 g (14 oz) tin peeled and diced roma tomatoes,
  or 4 fresh tomatoes, roughly chopped**
finely grated zest of 1 orange
extra-virgin olive oil for flavour

Dust the meat cubes with flour. Choose a saucepan with a lid that is large enough to hold all the ingredients without crowding; place it over a medium heat with 4 tablespoons of the olive oil. Add the meat, brown it a little, then remove it and set it to one side.

Add the remaining 2 tablespoons of oil to the saucepan, along with the garlic, rosemary, chilli, bay leaves, parsley stalks, sage, onions, celery and carrots. Sauté gently for about 15 minutes; stir often to prevent the vegetables sticking to the bottom.

Once the vegetables soften, return the meat to the pan and cook over a high heat. After about 5 minutes, add the wine; allow it to reduce a little, then add the stock (or water) and tomatoes.

Cover the pan, reduce the heat to a light simmer and cook for 2–3 hours. If the pan becomes dry, add more stock or water. Pull out a little piece of beef every now and then for testing: if it falls apart when you press it lightly, it's tender enough to serve.

Remove the pan from the stove, and add the parsley leaves, orange zest and a lug of extra-virgin olive oil; fold gently to combine the flavours. Serve with Polenta (see page 193) or Mashed Potatoes alla Tobie (see page 156) and a green salad.

Variations for wellbeing

Dairy intolerance, lactose intolerance – enjoy as is
Gluten intolerance – use maize cornflour instead of plain flour;
  use gluten-free breadcrumbs
IBS – omit the onions; use maize cornflour; reduce red wine by half

Under THE SEA

Crumbed swordfish with rosemary and chilli

Snapper baked in eggwhites with fennel, mint and lemon

Baked lobster with parsley, rosemary and chardonnay

Whole snapper with fennel seeds

Roasted tuna with cherry tomatoes, vermouth and basil

Poached ocean trout

Venetian crabs

Red mullet cooked with saffron, fennel and black olives

Seafood broth

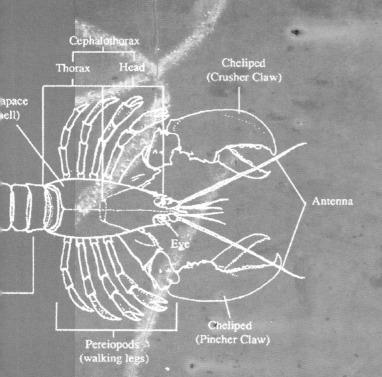

Cephalothorax

Thorax　　Head

Carapace
(shell)

Cheliped
(Crusher Claw)

Antenna

Eye

Cheliped
(Pincher Claw)

Pereiopods
(walking legs)

'... A GOOD FISHMONGER
IS YOUR BEST CHANCE OF
GETTING **THE FRESHEST**
AND MOST APPROPRIATE
SPECIES FOR A PARTICULAR
DISH, PREPARED IN THE WAY
THE RECIPE REQUIRES—
THEN ALL THAT'S LEFT IS
THE COOKING.'

When I first started working in kitchens, many moons ago, I had to clean upwards of 30 kilograms of fresh squid a day. Invariably, I'd start to smell like the sea-faring creatures I was spending so much time with, which tended to limit me a little on the social front.

Preparing seafood can be messy and unsettling. In a restaurant situation, I'll always start with a whole fish, because it's easier to judge its freshness: a good fresh fish won't be dehydrated from too much time out of the water; it will have clear eyes – no cloudiness at all; and a thin layer of slime will have formed on its scales.

But if it's Saturday morning and I'm buying for dinner, I'll tend to go for the ready-to-cook option: cleaned, scaled and, depending on the dish, filleted. The last thing I want to do is spend Saturday arvo getting that 'under the sea' smell out of the house.

If you're similarly disinclined, find a good fishmonger, and keep going back. Then you can take it on faith that a fish is fresh, rather than having to gaze into its eyes.

Buy fish on the day you intend to prepare it. This is particularly important when purchasing lobster or crab. These creatures are usually sold live, but I recommend you get the fishmonger to kill them on the spot. The correct method for humanely killing crabs and lobsters is rather involved, and the non-humane method – dropping them in boiling water – is not good for your karma.

After working in Europe for so long, it's been interesting writing recipes for species that are available here, but not in European waters, and vice versa. As an example, monkfish or stargazer, a wonderfully firm fish used a lot in England, is only found in one area of Australia, and while the fish look the same, they are remarkably different in taste. Wherever possible in this book, I've provided a few alternatives, but, as above, many of these quandries can be solved by getting cosy with your fishmonger.

Crumbed swordfish with rosemary and chilli

This is a cooking method that can be applied to all manner of ingredients, including most types of fish; meat, such as veal and lamb; and vegetables, such as eggplant and zucchini. You need skewers for this dish: metal or wooden ones are fine, or you could go rustic and use rosemary stalks. If you are using wooden skewers, make sure you soak them for about 15 minutes beforehand.

Serves 2

1 bay leaf
½ teaspoon dried chilli
sea salt
1 tablespoon rosemary leaves, roughly chopped
finely grated zest of 1 lemon
1 quantity Breadcrumbs (see page 190)
400 (14 oz) swordfish steaks, cut into
**   2 cm (¾ in) cubes**
freshly ground black pepper
2 free-range eggs, beaten
plain (all-purpose) flour for dusting
4–6 tablespoons olive oil

Use a mortar and pestle to smash the bay leaf, chilli and salt to a powder. Place the powder in a mixing bowl with the rosemary, lemon zest and breadcrumbs, and mix lightly.

Season the fish with salt and pepper. Have to hand the ingredients you'll need to crumb the fish: the beaten egg and a plate each of the flour and seasoned breadcrumbs. Flour the fish (shake to remove excess), dip it in the egg, then coat it in the breadcrumbs. Secure the breadcrumbs by pressing down on the cubes of fish with the tips of your fingers.

Slide the fish cubes onto skewers – about 4 per skewer. Heat the oil in a frying pan over a medium-to-high heat. Place the skewers

in the frying pan, and cook the fish quickly, making sure to brown on all sides. Drain on kitchen paper to remove excess oil.

I generally serve this dish with something really nice and simple. A handful of rocket will do it, or, for something a little fancier, try the Rocket, Fennel and Blood Orange Salad (see page 142).

Variations for wellbeing
Dairy intolerance, lactose intolerance – enjoy as is
Gluten intolerance, IBS – use maize cornflour instead of plain flour;
    use gluten-free breadcrumbs

Breadcrumbs

3

4 Oil

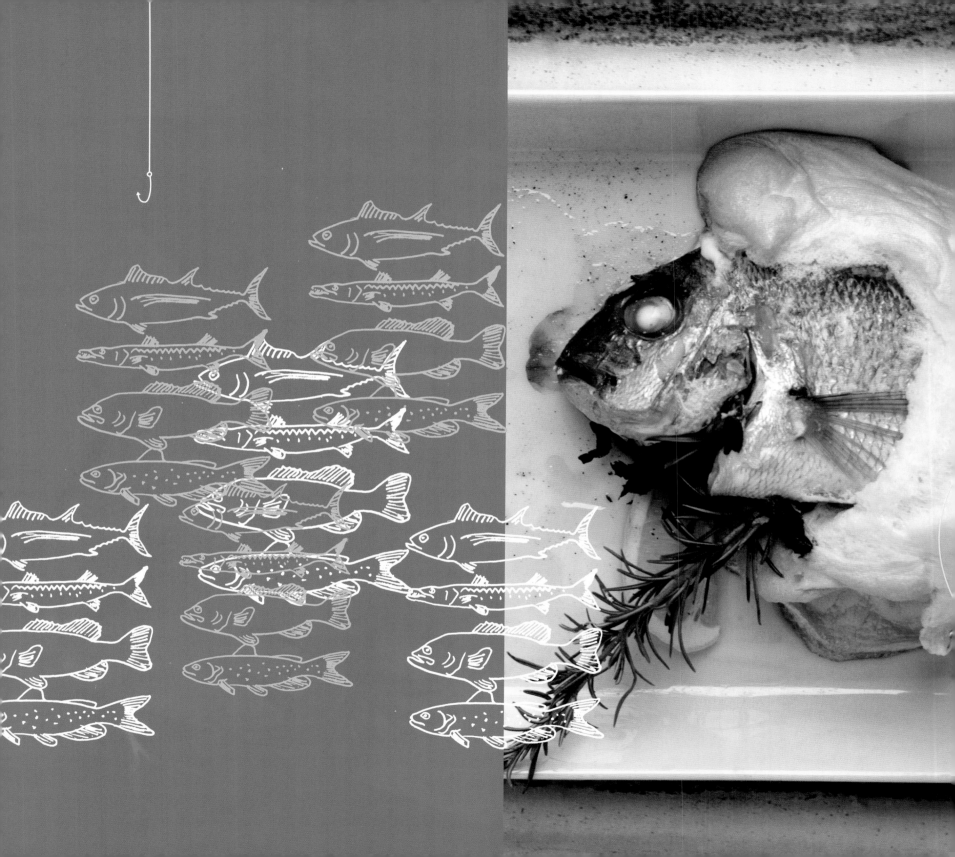

Snapper baked in eggwhites with fennel, mint and lemon

I often use eggwhites to make a crust within which to bake poultry or fish. This method is very similar to salt baking in that it traps the heat and flavour inside. Don't go eating the crust – eggwhites are fairly ordinary in the taste department.

You'll need about 10 eggwhites for this recipe. Rather than throwing away the separated yolks, use them to make Mayonnaise (see page 190), always a versatile accompaniment, or save the yolks for something sweet, such as Almond Custard (see page 169) or Crème Brûlée (see page 175).

Serves 2

**1 baby snapper, about 1 kg (2 lb),
    cleaned and scaled
sea salt
freshly ground black pepper
¼ bulb fennel, inner layers only, finely sliced
a small handful of mint
2 lemons, 1 sliced and 1 for juice
8–10 free-range eggwhites, at room temperature
oil for greasing
extra-virgin olive oil for flavour**

Preheat the oven to 220°C (430°C). Rinse the snapper under cold water and pat dry with kitchen paper.

Season the inside of the fish with salt and pepper, then stuff with the fennel, mint and lemon slices.

Place the eggwhites in a bowl and whisk until soft peaks form. Make sure your bowl and whisk are as dry as possible – extra moisture will make the whites flabby and watery.

Grease a baking tray with oil and lay the fish on the tray. Cover the exposed side of the fish with eggwhites to form an elongated mound. Bake in the oven for 20–30 minutes – until the eggwhites brown.

Remove from the oven. Allow the fish to sit for a few minutes before taking the eggwhite case off the fish. Drizzle the fish with extra-virgin olive oil and add a good squeeze of lemon. Serve whole with Cauliflower and Bottarga Salad (see page 144) or Green Vegetables, Braised (see page 190).

Variations for wellbeing
Dairy intolerance, gluten intolerance, IBS, lactose intolerance – enjoy as is

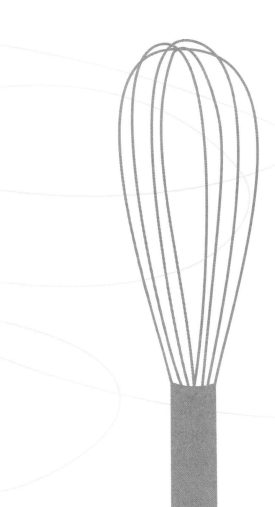

Baked lobster with parsley, rosemary and chardonnay

This recipe calls for a whole lobster, but you can easily substitute uncooked lobster tails, which are probably a little easier to work with if you're a crustacean novice. Ask your fishmonger to kill – but not cook – the lobster on the day you intend to prepare it.

Serves 1– 2

1 medium lobster (or lobster tail),
   killed but not cooked
sea salt
freshly ground black pepper
200 g (7 oz) butter
1 sprig rosemary, leaves removed and finely chopped
1 glass chardonnay
juice of ½ lemon
a handful of flat-leaf parsley, roughly chopped
extra-virgin olive oil for flavour

Variations for wellbeing
Gluten intolerance, lactose intolerance – enjoy as is
Dairy intolerance – use dairy-free margarine instead of butter
IBS – reduce butter and chardonnay

Preheat the oven to 180°C (360°F). With a sharp knife, slice the lobster in half, lengthways, then use your fingers to remove its intestines (these extend from the lobster's tail to its belly area and are a brownish colour). Season the flesh with salt and pepper.

Melt the butter in a flameproof and ovenproof dish, such as a casserole dish, over a medium heat. Add the lobster halves, with their flesh side facing up, and fry for a couple of minutes; sprinkle with rosemary and splash in the wine. Squeeze lemon juice over the flesh, then place the skin of the lemon in the pan. Transfer the dish from the stovetop to the oven.

The lobster will take about 10 minutes to cook. If in doubt, check the colour of the flesh: like fish, lobster flesh will gradually lose its translucency as it cooks and become white and opaque.

Transfer the lobster to a serving dish, scatter with parsley and add a generous drizzle of olive oil. Serve with rocket leaves or a mixed-herb salad.

Whole snapper with fennel seeds

I've used snapper here, which is a tasty fish with a lovely pinkish tinge to its flesh. If I was in the UK, I would probably use baby bass.

Serves 4

olive oil for greasing
1 baby snapper, about 1.5 kg (3¼ lb),
 cleaned and scaled
2 large sprigs rosemary, leaves only
4 cloves garlic, peeled
1 teaspoon fennel seeds
100 g (3½ oz) prosciutto
sea salt
freshly ground black pepper
extra-virgin olive oil for flavour
juice of ½ lemon

Preheat the oven to 200°C (400°F). Grease a large baking tray. Rinse the snapper in cold water and pat dry with kitchen paper.

Place the rosemary, garlic, fennel seeds and prosciutto in a food processor, and blitz until you have a nice coarse paste. Season with salt and pepper. Stuff the cavity of the fish with the paste and smooth any remaining mixture over the skin of the fish.

Place the fish in the oven for 20–30 minutes. Combine the extra-virgin olive oil and lemon juice, then use it to baste the fish as it cooks.

Serve the fish whole, at the table, with Salsa Dragoncella (see page 193) and a salad of greens.

Variations for wellbeing
Dairy intolerance, gluten intolerance, IBS, lactose intolerance – enjoy as is

Roasted tuna with cherry tomatoes, vermouth and basil

Tuna is a lovely big, thick fish. If you try to cook it all the way through, it will toughen up. Like a good piece of beef, tuna should be pink on the inside when it comes to the table.

Serves 4

olive oil for greasing
4 × 180 g (6 oz) tuna steaks
sea salt
freshly ground black pepper
500 g (1 lb) cherry tomatoes
2 cloves garlic, finely sliced
1 tablespoon small capers
1½ glasses vermouth or dry white wine
a handful of basil leaves

Preheat the oven to 180°C (360°F). Choose a baking dish large enough to hold all the tuna fillets without crowding and grease with a little oil. Season both sides of the tuna with salt and pepper, and arrange the fillets in the baking dish.

Cut the tomatoes in half; using a spoon or your fingers, remove and discard the seeds. Place the tomato flesh in a bowl with the garlic, capers, vermouth and basil. Mix lightly, then arrange over the tuna. Cover the fish with foil, and bake in the oven for 10–20 minutes. Baste a couple of times with the juices from the bottom of the dish.

Serve the tuna nice and hot, with a generous dollop of the tomato mixture from the bottom of the baking dish.

Variations for wellbeing
Dairy intolerance, gluten intolerance, lactose intolerance – enjoy as is
IBS – use Fish Stock (see page 195) instead of vermouth or wine

Roasted Tuna with Cherry Tomatoes, Vermouth and Basil

Poached ocean trout

Poaching is a wonderfully healthy way to cook a whole fish.
You'll need a fish kettle or other long flameproof pan. Ocean trout
is used here, but this recipe works very well with a range of fish,
including salmon. Any leftovers can be kept in the fridge for
a few days, and then served cold with aïoli (see Mayonnaise,
page 190) and asparagus spears.

Serves 4–6

**1 ocean trout, about 1.5 kg (3¼ lb),
  cleaned and scaled
1 leek, roughly chopped
1 onion, roughly chopped
1 carrot, roughly chopped
1 stick celery, roughly chopped
a handful of flat-leaf parsley
10 peppercorns
2 chillies, halved (optional)**

Rinse the fish under cold water and pat dry with kitchen paper.

Put all the ingredients in the fish kettle (or other suitable pan),
and cover with water. Bring the water to a fast simmer, then turn
the heat down to a gentle simmer. Cook for about 25 minutes.

As soon as the fish is done (test with a skewer), lift it out of the
water to prevent further cooking. Discard the other ingredients.
Remove the fish's head, backbone and skin. Arrange on plates.
Serve with a Salsa Dragoncella (see page 193).

Variations for wellbeing
Dairy intolerance, gluten intolerance, lactose intolerance – enjoy as is
IBS – omit onion and leek and double amount of celery and carrot

Venetian crabs

I like to cook crabs in actual sea water. If it's not readily available, I'll do a fair imitation by adding heaps of salt to the cooking water.

When buying the crabs, select a nice meaty variety. What's available will depend largely on the season and location. Ask your fishmonger to kill – but not cook – the crabs on the day you intend to prepare them.

Serves 4

500 g (1 lb 2 oz) rock salt
4 crabs, about 600 g (1¼ lb) each,
**   killed but not cooked**
finely grated zest and juice of 1 lemon
3 tablespoons extra-virgin olive oil,
**   plus extra for flavour**
1 teaspoon freshly chopped chilli
1 tablespoon roughly chopped parsley
1 tablespoon finely sliced mint
½ quantity Breadcrumbs (see page 190)
sea salt
freshly ground black pepper
a small handful of celery leaves

Add the 2 cups of rock salt to a very large saucepan (or stockpot) of water (about 65 g (2½ oz) of salt per 1 litre of water). Bring the water to a boil. Add the crabs and cook for about 10 minutes. Remove the crabs and allow to cool.

Preheat the griller to medium. Insert the tip of a strong knife in the underside of each crab, just under the eyes, and lever out the central section of the bottom shell. Remove the top shell (over the head) and set aside for later use. Take all the white flesh out of the shells, discarding the feathery grey gills. The brownish-yellow head meat can be kept and used if you like a really strong fishy taste. Cut the white flesh into small pieces and place it in a bowl with the head meat

(if using). Add the lemon zest and juice, 3 tablespoons of extra-virgin olive oil, chilli, parsley, mint and breadcrumbs (don't overdo it on the crumbs – a small handful per crab), and season with salt and pepper.

Wash and dry the empty head shells and fill them with the crab-flesh mixture. Place the shells under the griller until the surface of the crab mixture starts to brown.

Serve with a drizzle of extra-virgin olive oil and a scatter of celery leaves. Saffron mayonnaise (see Mayonnaise, page 190) works nicely with this dish.

Variations for wellbeing
Dairy intolerance, lactose intolerance – enjoy as is
Gluten intolerance, IBS – use gluten-free breadcrumbs

Red mullet cooked with saffron, fennel and black olives

In this recipe the fish is cooked in a 'bag', or, more precisely, a parcel fashioned from aluminium foil. The recipe calls for a smallish fish known as red mullet (other names include goatfish and barbounia), but a variety of small fish are suitable (and may be more readily available), such as garfish. The idea of using smaller fish is that each of your guests gets a couple of whole fish apiece. Ask your fishmonger what's good on the day.

Serves 2

**4 small- to medium-sized red mullet,
   cleaned and scaled**
½ glass chardonnay
a pinch of saffron threads
2 bay leaves
2 cloves garlic, finely sliced
1 tablespoon extra-virgin olive oil
½ bulb fennel, tough outer layer removed
olive oil for greasing
2 tablespoons black olives, stoned
sea salt
freshly ground black pepper
finely chopped flat-leaf parsley to garnish

Preheat the oven to 200°C (400°F). Rinse the fish under cold water and pat dry with kitchen paper.

In a small bowl, combine the chardonnay, saffron, bay leaves, garlic and extra-virgin olive oil; leave the bowl in a warm place to allow the flavours to infuse.

Slice the fennel as finely as possible. Soak it in cold water for about 5 minutes, then drain.

Take 2 large pieces of aluminium foil and grease lightly with olive oil. Arrange 2 fish on each piece of foil. Scatter the olives and the fennel evenly between the parcels. Draw the edges of the foil up around

the fish to make a bowl shape, one capable of holding liquid (do not close the tops of the parcels yet), then place in a baking dish, side by side. Pour the chardonnay and saffron infusion over the fish, and season with salt and pepper. Crimple the foil to seal each bag closed. Bake in the oven for 12–15 minutes.

Remove the baking dish from the oven, and allow the foil parcels to sit unopened for a few minutes. When you do open them, watch out for the sudden blast of steam.

Use a spatula to arrange the fish on plates. Scoop the mixture from the foil parcels – the fennel, olives and juices – and drizzle over the fish. Garnish with parsley. Serve immediately with Green Vegetables, Braised (see page 190) or a green salad.

Variations for wellbeing
Dairy intolerance, gluten intolerance, IBS, lactose intolerance – enjoy as is

Seafood broth

Known in Italy as brodetto di pesce, this flavoursome dish is more like a stew than a soup. The liquid that forms comes from the juices of the seafood, wine and tomatoes, rather than stock. This is one of the first dishes I learnt to cook at Caffé e Cucina. It's wonderfully versatile: most European countries have a version, and every cook who makes it more than once adjusts the recipe to their own taste.

Serves 2

200 g (7 oz) clams
200 g (7 oz) mussels
4 prawns or scampi
2 small crabs, killed but not cooked
6 tomatoes
2 tablespoons olive oil
2 cloves garlic, finely sliced
1 bunch flat-leaf parsley, stalks finely chopped
   and leaves roughly chopped
3 anchovy fillets
1 fresh red chilli, finely sliced
200 g (7 oz) firm-fleshed white-fish fillets,
   cut into 2 cm (¾ in) cubes
½ glass chardonnay or other white wine
1 squid tube, cut into 5 mm (¼ in) rings

Rinse the clams and mussels under cold water. Remove the beard from the mussels – a sharp tug usually does it. If necessary, scrape off any barnacles by using the sharp end of one mussel against the shell of another. Prepare the prawns by removing the heads, if you wish, then slicing their bodies in half – cut from head to tail along the back; finally, remove the vein. To split the crabs, remove the top shells (just peel off with your hands), remove the grey feathery gills, then, with your hands, break the body in half down the middle.

Quarter the tomatoes and remove the seeds, using your fingers or a teaspoon. Discard the seeds and keep the flesh.

Heat the oil over a medium heat in a saucepan large enough to hold all the ingredients, then gently sauté the garlic, parsley stalks (put the parsley leaves to one side), anchovies, chilli and tomatoes for about 2 minutes.

Add the crabs. Cover the saucepan and cook for 2 minutes before adding the fish, clams, mussels and prawns. Cover again, and cook for a minute or so.

Add the wine, cover, and cook for another couple of minutes. Add the squid and remove the saucepan from the heat. Allow it to sit with its lid on for about 5 minutes (the residual heat will cook the squid).

Sprinkle the broth with the parsley leaves. If your cooking pot is presentable, take it straight to the table. Otherwise, put the broth in a large serving bowl (warm it up a little first). Serve with plenty of warm crusty bread.

Variations for wellbeing
Dairy intolerance, gluten intolerance, IBS, lactose intolerance – enjoy as is

ON THE SIDE

Rocket, fennel and blood orange salad

Cauliflower and bottarga salad

Mixed tomato salad with ricotta, marjoram and balsamic vinegar

Baked fennel with cream, pancetta and parmesan

Beetroot, horseradish, marjoram and crème fraîche salad

Potato rosti

Cabbage with garlic and anchovies

Mustard fruits

Mashed potatoes alla Tobie

Roasted potatoes with milk, rosemary garlic

Warm spinach salad with pine nuts and balsamic vinegar

'THE RECIPES THAT FOLLOW, MOSTLY VEGIES + SALADS, ARE MORE OR LESS THE OTHER HALF OF THE FISH AND MEAT CHAPTERS. WHILE I'VE MADE A FEW SUGGESTIONS HERE AND THERE ABOUT WHAT GOES NICELY WITH WHAT, **NOTHING IS SET IN CONCRETE** - IT'S UP TO YOU.'

I remember watching my partner, the lovely Georgia, flicking through a cookbook and dismissing heaps of recipes because she didn't dig fennel or there was too much chilli or she couldn't stomach cannellini beans. Many cookbooks 'package' meals – so you get your chicken with couscous, or beef with garlic mash – that sort of thing. But because I live with a fussy eater, and because I know, from twenty-odd years of living with my dad, how literal people can be when it comes to recipes, I have decided to separate things out a bit. So you don't have to ditch the beef and mash, just because you are allergic to potatoes; instead, you can cook the beef, but pair it with fennel or beetroot or whatever takes your fancy.

The best thing about a mix and match approach, apart from the fun of experimenting, is that it's very season friendly. Serving a steak with mashed potatoes, as compared to a rocket salad, will completely change the structure of the dish, turning a summer meal into a winter one.

In the interests of even greater flexibility, and at the risk of further confusing my dad, I'm going to go out on a limb and say that many of the dishes here don't need to be thought of as mere 'sides', but will do very nicely as meals, snacks or starters. You'll find that a cauliflower and bottarga salad is a worthy addition to a selection of antipasto; a spinach salad will always shape up well as a light lunch; and baked fennel makes an exceptional late supper, particularly if accompanied by a big glass of red.

Obviously, vegetables are the star feature of the following dishes, so here's a bit of advice on getting good quality. Whenever possible, buy local. If the only fennel available on the day comes from halfway around the world, cook a different dish. Buy organic if you can, and shop at fresh-food markets and small fruiterers. For those who heed this advice, a word of warning: the taste of good vegies is addictive. Once you're used to the big, earthy, complex flavours of really fresh seasonal produce, you'll eat vegies because you love 'em, and not because your mum told you to!

Rocket, fennel and blood orange salad

This is a classic salad. The pairing of citrus with the sharp aniseed flavour of fennel is a real love match. If you can't find blood oranges, substitute any variety of orange or mandarin.

Variations for wellbeing
Dairy intolerance, gluten intolerance, IBS, lactose intolerance – enjoy as is

Serves 2

1 blood orange
½ large bulb fennel
2 handfuls of rocket (arugula)
10 mint leaves
10 flat-leaf parsley leaves
2 tablespoons extra-virgin olive oil
sea salt
freshly ground black pepper

Grate the orange zest using a zester or a fine grater. Squeeze the orange just enough to collect a couple of teaspoons of juice, and add the juice to the grated zest. Peel the pith from the orange and cut the flesh into segments.

Remove the core and tough outer layer of the fennel. Slice the bulb as finely as possible – you can use a potato peeler for this – then soak the slices in iced water.

Trim the rocket of any roots and excess stalks. Rinse the rocket, mint and parsley leaves. Dry the leaves in a salad spinner, or drain them on kitchen paper.

To make the dressing, place the olive oil, orange zest and juice, and salt and pepper in a mixing bowl, and stir lightly to combine.

Place the rocket and herb leaves and the orange segments in a salad bowl. Drain the fennel slices and shake them a little to get rid of excess water. Add the fennel to the salad bowl. Drizzle the dressing over the leaves; toss and serve.

Cauliflower and bottarga salad

Bottarga is dried, salted fish roe. The best bottarga comes in a small block and is available from specialist Italian stores and other gourmet outlets. Don't buy it in a powder or paste form; if you can't get the real stuff, use anchovies, which are similarly salty and fishy – about 4 fillets should do for this recipe.

Serves 4

1 small cauliflower
4 tablespoons white-wine vinegar
1 fresh red chilli, seeded and sliced
extra-virgin olive oil
a small handful of flat-leaf parsley,
** roughly chopped**
freshly ground black pepper
a small handful of pale celery leaves
** (from centre of bunch)**
finely grated bottarga

Bring a large saucepan of salted water to a boil. Use a sharp knife to remove the cauliflower florets. Plunge the florets into the boiling water and cook for about 2 minutes. Drain and rinse under cold water.

Combine the cauliflower, vinegar, chilli, olive oil, parsley and pepper in a good-sized serving bowl. Toss to ensure the florets are well coated with the dressing. Scatter with the celery leaves and finish with finely grated bottarga.

Variations for wellbeing
Dairy intolerance, gluten intolerance, IBS, lactose intolerance – enjoy as is

Mixed tomato salad with ricotta, marjoram and balsamic vinegar

This salad gets really interesting when there's a mix of colour, flavour and texture, so try to use a couple of different varieties of tomato, or tomatoes at different stages of the ripening process. If you use the smaller varieties, such as cherry and grape tomatoes, adjust your amounts. Make this salad in the late summer when tomatoes are at their cheapest and best. Ahead of preparation, warm the tomatoes a little by sitting them in the sun for 15 minutes.

Serves 2

200 g (7 oz) ricotta
sea salt
freshly ground black pepper
olive oil for baking
5 tomatoes of mixed variety
a small handful of marjoram or basil
balsamic vinegar for dressing
extra-virgin olive oil for dressing

Preheat the oven to 180°C (360°F).

Crumble the ricotta onto a baking tray; season with salt and pepper and drizzle with a little olive oil. Bake in the oven until golden; remove and set aside to cool.

Cut the tomatoes into bite-sized pieces and place them in a salad bowl with the marjoram (or basil), a splash of balsamic vinegar, salt and pepper, and a generous lug of extra-virgin olive oil. Give the mixture a good toss to ensure the tomatoes are well coated.

Arrange the tomatoes on a serving plate, scatter with the baked ricotta and season with a good grind of black pepper.

Variations for wellbeing
Gluten intolerance – enjoy as is
Dairy intolerance – use goat's or sheep's cheese instead of ricotta
IBS, lactose intolerance – half serves only

Baked fennel with cream, pancetta and parmesan

This is one of the most indulgent fennel recipes you're ever likely to find. It's off-limits if you're on a diet, but an absolute must if you're a lover of strong, creamy flavours. Team this one with something simple, such as roasted meat or fish. The recipe also works well with potatoes.

Serves 4

2 large or 4–5 small bulbs fennel
plain (all-purpose) flour for dusting
100 g (3½ oz) butter, plus extra for greasing
150 g (5 oz) pancetta
4 tablespoons double cream
sea salt
freshly ground black pepper
150 g (5 oz) freshly grated parmesan cheese

Bring a large saucepan of salted water to a boil.

Remove and discard the thick outer layers of the fennel. Cut the bulbs into 3 cm (1¼ in) slices – retain a bit of stalk at the end.

Place the fennel in the boiling water and cook until tender. Drain and pat dry with kitchen paper. Preheat the oven to 190°C (375°F).

Dust the fennel with flour. Melt half the butter in a large frying pan, then add the fennel. Cook over a medium heat. Once the fennel is golden on all sides, add the pancetta, and cook for a minute or two. Add the cream, then season with salt and pepper. Reduce the heat to a low simmer, and cook for a further 10 minutes.

Grease a baking dish with butter. Arrange the fennel in the dish and drizzle with the remaining cream from the frying pan. Sprinkle the fennel with parmesan and dabs of the remaining butter. Cook in the oven for about 15 minutes or until the parmesan melts. Serve immediately.

Variations for wellbeing

Lactose intolerance – enjoy as is

Dairy intolerance – use goat's or sheep's cheese instead of parmesan; use goat's crème fraîche instead of cream; use dairy-free margarine instead of butter

Gluten intolerance, IBS – use maize cornflour instead of plain flour

Beetroot, horseradish, marjoram and crème fraîche salad

In this brightly coloured salad, the rich, full beetroot taste is tempered by the tang of citrus and the heat of horseradish. Serve the dish on its own or with grilled or roasted meat. Hang onto your beetroot leaves: they can be steamed or braised as you would spinach, or used to make a tasty pasta filling.

Variations for wellbeing

Gluten intolerance, IBS, lactose intolerance – enjoy as is

Dairy intolerance – use goat's milk crème fraîche

Serves 2

5 medium beetroots, golden or purple
1 tablespoon freshly grated horseradish
1 tablespoon marjoram leaves
freshly grated zest and juice of ½ lemon
a handful of flat-leaf parsley, finely chopped
sea salt
freshly ground black pepper
3 tablespoons extra-virgin olive oil
2 heaped tablespoons crème fraîche
20 pale celery leaves (from centre of bunch)

Rinse the beetroots in cold water and scrub them with a small brush to remove any grit. Place the beetroots in a saucepan and fill with cold water and a pinch of salt. Bring to a boil, then reduce to a simmer. Cook until the beetroots are quite tender; use a skewer to test.

Drain well and set aside until the beetroots are cool to touch. Use a knife or your fingers to remove their skins – this should be fairly easy. Cut each beetroot into about 6 pieces and place in a salad bowl. Add the horseradish, marjoram, lemon zest, parsley, salt and pepper, and olive oil; give the beets a good stir to ensure all the pieces are thoroughly coated with the dressing.

In a small bowl, combine the lemon juice and crème fraîche and add a grind of black pepper, then drizzle the mixture over the beets. Scatter with celery leaves, and serve.

Potato rosti

Rosti – grated-potato pancakes – are a staple of the German-speaking countries of Europe. When I was living in Switzerland, I ate rosti every day, with pungent cheese or cured meats or sausage. I'd pretty much overdosed on the stuff by the time I left, but recently the cravings have returned.

Serves 4

1 kg (2 lb) potatoes, whole and unpeeled
1 onion, very finely sliced
sea salt
freshly ground black pepper
125 ml (4 fl oz) olive oil

Put the whole potatoes into a large saucepan of salted water. Bring to a boil, and cook until the flesh can be pierced easily with a skewer. Drain the potatoes and rinse under cold water.

Allow the potatoes to cool, then grate them into a large bowl. Add the onion, and salt and pepper, and mix thoroughly.

Heat some of the oil – about 1 cm (½ in) – in a frying pan over a medium-to-high heat. Add 1 heaped tablespoon of the potato mixture and press down to form a little cake. Make enough of these to fill but not crowd the pan. Fry until the rosti are golden on both sides. Drain on kitchen paper, and keep warm in a low oven. Add the next batch to the frying pan, and follow the same method until you have used all the mixture. As you fry, add more oil and adjust the heat as necessary.

Arrange on a platter. Serve hot with cured meats or cheese, or as a side dish.

Variations for wellbeing
Dairy intolerance, gluten intolerance, lactose intolerance – enjoy as is
IBS – omit onion

Cabbage with garlic and anchovies

This full-flavoured dish can also be made using Tuscan kale, a member of the cabbage family. The dish is a winner when paired with a pork chop and will also smarten up a piece of roast beef or a serve of sausages.

Serves 4

1 head savoy cabbage
2–3 tablespoons olive oil
2 cloves garlic, finely sliced
2 bay leaves
4 anchovy fillets
white-wine vinegar for flavour
freshly ground black pepper

Remove and discard the tough outer leaves of the cabbage. Break the inner leaves into smallish pieces.

Heat the oil in a large frying pan. Add the sliced leaves, along with the garlic and bay leaves. Sauté over a medium heat, stirring frequently.

Add the anchovies to the pan. Turn the heat to low and cook for about 15 minutes or until the leaves start to soften.

Add a good splash of white-wine vinegar. Continue cooking until most of the liquid has evaporated; season with pepper, and serve hot.

Variations for wellbeing
Dairy intolerance, gluten intolerance, IBS, lactose intolerance – enjoy as is

Cabbage with Garlic and Anchovies

Mustard fruits

The sweet, slightly candied taste of these preserved fruits is undercut by a nice sharp hit of mustard. Traditionally the fruits are served with boiled meats (bollito misto), although I have used them with success in ravioli and risotto dishes, and alongside grilled or oven-roasted meat.

Makes 3 × 500 ml (1 pint) jars

**1.5 kg (3¼ lb) fresh mixed fruits (apples,
  pears, peaches, apricots, grapes, cherries)
3 x 350 g (12 oz) jars honey
finely grated zest and juice of 1 lemon
1½ glasses white wine
100g (3½ oz) mustard seeds**

Choose wide-necked jars suitable for preserving, and sterilise (see page 194). Wash the fruit well, then dry. Prepare the different fruit as necessary: core the apples and pears; stone the apricots and peaches. Cherries and grapes are okay used whole.

Put the larger fruit into a saucepan big enough to hold all the ingredients, and cover with cold water. Add 1 tablespoon of honey and the zest and juice of the lemon. Bring to a simmer and cook for about 30 minutes. Add the smaller fruit; cook for about 5 minutes, then remove from the heat and allow to cool.

In a second saucepan, add the wine and the rest of the honey, and bring to a gentle simmer. Reduce the liquid by ⅓, then add the mustard seeds. Remove from the heat and allow to cool.

Combine the 2 lots of ingredients, and mix carefully to avoid breaking the fruit. Place the fruit in the sterilised jars; seal the jars well and refrigerate. The fruit will keep for up to a year.

Variations for wellbeing
Dairy intolerance, gluten intolerance, lactose intolerance – enjoy as is
IBS – not suitable

Mashed potatoes alla Tobie

Mashed potato is seen as rather ordinary, but I reckon it's one of the best dishes around. Part of its charm is its versatility. You can add a huge number of ingredients for flavour and texture: cod, garlic, cream, celeriac, eggs – to name a few. Personally, I reckon you can't go past the basics: milk plus olive oil or butter. In this recipe I've added a flavour hit in the form of parmesan and nutmeg.

Serves 2

4 medium floury potatoes, peeled
1 clove garlic, finely chopped
a pinch of nutmeg
2 tablespoons freshly grated parmesan cheese
4 tablespoons milk
sea salt
freshly ground black pepper
2 tablespoons extra-virgin olive oil

Cut each potato into 8 pieces and place in a large saucepan filled with salted water. Bring to a boil, cooking the potatoes until they are quite soft.

Drain the potatoes, then mash them, using either a potato masher or potato ricer (this looks and works like a garlic crusher). Add the garlic, nutmeg, parmesan, milk, salt and pepper, and olive oil. Mix the ingredients well. If you like, use a whisk to give the mash a light, fluffy texture.

Variations for wellbeing

Gluten intolerance, IBS, lactose intolerance – enjoy as is

Dairy intolerance – use goat's or sheep's cheese instead of parmesan; use goat's or sheep's milk instead of regular milk

Roasted potatoes with milk, rosemary and garlic

The milk in this recipe is the key. It curdles as it heats, creating a tasty coating around the potatoes. Use full-cream milk for this one; the low-fat varieties tend to go watery when heated.

Serves 4

250 ml (9 fl oz) milk
2 tablespoons rosemary, roughly chopped
4 garlic cloves, finely sliced
olive oil for greasing
6 medium potatoes, peeled
sea salt
freshly ground black pepper

In a bowl large enough to hold all the ingredients, combine the milk, rosemary and garlic; set aside for 20 minutes to allow the flavours to get acquainted.

Preheat the oven to 200°C (400°F) and grease a baking tray with a little olive oil.

Cut the potatoes into slices 5 mm (¼ in) thick and add them to the bowl with the milk. Season with salt and pepper. Use a large wooden spoon or your hands to fold the potatoes into the milk mixture.

Lay the potatoes on the baking tray in rows – a little bit of overlap is fine, but not too much. Cook in the oven for about 30 minutes. Flip occasionally to make sure the slices brown evenly. Serve hot.

Variations for wellbeing

Gluten intolerance, IBS – enjoy as is

Dairy intolerance – use goat's or sheep's milk instead of regular milk

Lactose intolerance – use lactose-free milk instead of regular milk

Roasted Potatoes with Milk,
Rosemary and Garlic

Warm spinach salad with pine nuts and balsamic vinegar

You'll never have to travel far to find a spinach salad on a restaurant menu. I first prepared a version during my apprenticeship days at Caffé e Cucina. This version relies on the sharp, sweet tang of balsamic vinegar for its flavour.

Serves 2

1 large bunch spinach
2 tablespoons olive oil
1 small onion, finely sliced
1 clove garlic, finely sliced
1 fresh red chilli, seeded
   and finely chopped
1 tablespoon pine nuts
2 tablespoons balsamic vinegar

Remove and discard the lower half of the spinach stalks. Rinse the spinach thoroughly in cold water, then drain and set aside.

Select a large frying pan or wok. Heat the oil over a low heat. Sauté the onion, garlic and chilli until the mixture is soft and translucent.

Raise the heat to medium. Add the pine nuts and cook until golden. Turn the heat to high, and add the spinach. Cook very briefly, just until the leaves begin to wilt, then add the balsamic vinegar. Stir to ensure the leaves are well coated with the vinegar.

Transfer the spinach to a bowl and serve warm as a starter or a side dish.

Variations for wellbeing
Dairy intolerance, gluten intolerance, lactose intolerance – enjoy as is
IBS – omit onion

Sweet!

Apple strudel

Ricotta fritters

Strawberries with balsamic vinegar

Almond custard

Crostoli

Battered and fried apple

Crème brûlée

Peaches baked with amaretto

Zabaglione served chilled

Fresh fig and pecorino seadas

Cherry pie

Panettone

Bomboloni – Italian doughnuts

Chocolate and olive oil tart

'THE TRADEMARK CULINARY **BRILLIANCE**
THAT WE ASSOCIATE WITH TYPICALLY
ITALIAN FOODS SUCH AS PASTA IS THERE
IN SPADES WHEN IT COMES TO SWEET TREATS'.

On my first visit to Italy, a friend picked me up at the Milan airport and drove me to Lake Como, where I had a job lined up. It was quite an experience, whizzing down those stunning hills towards the lake, past the holiday mansions of the rich and famous. But the highlight was the small cafe we stopped at for an espresso. The coffee was great, but it was the pastries that really impressed: small, fresh, beautifully presented explosions of flavour.

You might say, that's what you'd expect of the cafes in a resort town like Lake Como. But the point, as I was to discover, is that you'll find the same quality replicated the length and breadth of Italy – be it in the signature cafes of the stylish cities or in a railway cafe of some tiny rural town.

I love most Italian sweet treats, but my preference is for what I'll call street or cafe food – delectable pastries such as bomboloni, seadas and crostoli. These can be eaten at any time of the day: first thing in the morning with your coffee, midmorning, afternoon, even for dessert when paired with a scoop of ice cream or a dollop of custard.

In my experience, Italians are not ones for those big, structured desserts with complex flavours, although they have borrowed something of that tradition from the countries they share borders with. In the north, for example, you'll see a lot of fancy things done with apple, a nod to Italy's northern neighbour, Switzerland. Traditional French desserts such as crème brûlée often put in an appearance on menus in Italy, but then again, these are desserts with a universal appeal.

The recipes that follow are a bit of a mix, and reflect my own preferences. I love the simplicity of dishes that can be thrown together when unexpected guests rap at the door – things such as strawberries warmed in balsamic vinegar. But I also don't mind the challenge of marathon desserts: the ones that take a few hours to prepare, set and cook, and which are bound to impress on the night.

Apple strudel

The strudel I ate as a kid was always made with flaky puff pastry. When I was in Switzerland I discovered the delights of strudel made with a very thin, yeast-free, flour-and-water pastry.

The Swiss roll their strudels as they do their Swiss rolls: instead of the pastry being folded *over* the apple mixture it is rolled up *within* the mixture so as to create a lovely spiral effect.

Serves 6–10

100 g (3½ oz) raisins
125 ml (4fl oz) rum or brandy
1 tablespoon olive oil, plus extra for greasing
300 g (10 oz) plain flour,
  plus extra for dusting
a pinch of fine-grained salt
3 free-range eggs
1.5 kg (3¼ lb) apples, peeled, cored and thinly sliced
100 g (3½ oz) slivered almonds
100 g (3½ oz) castor sugar
a pinch of ground cinnamon
juice of 1 lemon
½ quantity Breadcrumbs (see page 190)
icing sugar for dusting

Soak the raisins in the rum or brandy. Preheat the oven to 180°C (360°F) and grease a large baking tray with a little oil.

Put the flour, salt, olive oil and one of the eggs into a large mixing bowl, along with about 85 ml (3 fl oz) of warm water. Using your hands, mix the ingredients together until they combine to form a soft dough. Turn the dough out onto a clean, flour-dusted surface, then knead the dough until it's smooth and elastic. Cover and put to one side. Don't bother wiping down the floured surface – you'll use it later.

Wipe out the mixing bowl. Place the rum-soaked raisins, apples, almonds, castor sugar, cinnamon and lemon juice in the bowl, and fold to combine. Put to one side.

Roll the dough on the floured surface. Aim for a thickness of around 3 mm (⅛ in). If the dough bunches up around the edges, trim with a sharp knife.

Scatter the breadcrumbs across the dough, then spread the apple mixture evenly. Roll the dough to form a classic strudel shape – plump and elongated. Secure the ends by folding the pastry over on itself, like an envelope. If the roll is too long to fit onto your baking tray, slice the strudel in half, and seal the edges as above.

Place the strudel on the baking tray. Beat the two remaining eggs in a small bowl, then, using a pastry brush, glaze the pastry. Place the strudel in the oven and bake until the pastry turns golden brown – about 30 minutes.

Dust with icing sugar, and serve hot with ice cream or Almond Custard (see page 169).

Variations for wellbeing
Dairy intolerance, lactose intolerance – enjoy as is
Gluten intolerance, IBS – not suitable

Ricotta fritters

People are likely to fall in love with you if you cook them these fritters – that's how good they are. They are best served hot but can be eaten cold – although they may get a bit soggy if kept for too long.

Makes about 20

400 g (14 oz) fresh ricotta
3 free-range eggs
5 tablespoons castor sugar
finely grated zest of 1 lemon
a pinch of bicarbonate of soda
3 tablespoons sultanas
200 g (7 oz) plain flour
500 ml (18 fl oz) vegetable oil
icing sugar for dusting

Drain the ricotta of excess moisture and place it in a large mixing bowl with the eggs; beat until smooth. Add the sugar, lemon zest, bicarbonate of soda, sultanas and flour; stir well to combine the ingredients. Cover with plastic film and rest the dough in the fridge for about 1 hour.

Set out a plate lined with kitchen paper. Heat the oil in a heavy-based saucepan. Test the heat by dropping in a pinch of flour: if it starts to sizzle, the oil is ready to fry. Use a tablespoon to scoop out dollops of the dough mix and drop them into the oil. Depending on the size of your saucepan, you'll probably be able to fry just a few fritters at a time. Cook until the fritters turn a nice golden brown, then drain well on kitchen paper.

Dust with icing sugar and serve piping hot.

Variations for wellbeing

Dairy intolerance – use goat's milk crème fraîche instead of ricotta
Gluten intolerance, IBS – use 4 tablespoons each of maize cornflour and rice flour and 2 tablespoons of soy flour, instead of plain flour; use pure icing sugar for dusting; small serves only
Lactose intolerance – suitable only if eaten in half serves

Strawberries with Balsamic Vinegar

Strawberries with balsamic vinegar

These are great on their own, but they also pair up nicely with desserts such as Almond Custard (see right) and Zabaglione Served Chilled (see page 179). Don't be put off by the vinegar in this recipe – once it combines with a bit of sugar and the heat from the oven, it takes on a wonderfully sweet and complex flavour.

Serves 2

1 punnet strawberries, hulled
1 tablespoon castor sugar
1 tablespoon balsamic vinegar

Preheat the oven to 200°C (400°F). If the strawberries are on the large size, cut them in half. Combine all the ingredients in a bowl.

Tear off a large piece of aluminium foil – it will need to be about 40 cm (16 in) in length. Fold the foil in half and make a 2 cm (¾ in) fold along each side, but not at the top (aim for an envelope shape).

Place the strawberry mixture inside the foil parcel, and make a fold along the top to secure. Place the parcel in the oven and cook for 5 minutes. Remove from the oven, and let the parcel sit, unopened, for a few minutes.

Serve at the table. The aroma that's released when the parcel is opened is really something special. Arrange the warm strawberries in martini or wine glasses, accompanied by a generous dollop of crème fraîche or custard.

Variations for wellbeing
Dairy intolerance, gluten intolerance, lactose intolerance – enjoy as is
IBS – suitable only if eaten in small serves

Almond custard

This delicious custard has a grown-up flavour that goes brilliantly with all manner of things, including fruit, tarts, strudels and cakes. It's also great just on its own.

Serves 2–4

500 ml (18 fl oz) milk
4 free-range egg yolks
4 tablespoons sugar
finely grated zest of 1 lemon
50 g (2 oz) ground almonds

Put the milk in a saucepan. Bring to a boil, then remove from the heat; cover to keep warm.

Choose a mixing bowl and saucepan of approximately the same size – the bowl has to fit comfortably on top of the saucepan. Half fill the saucepan with water and bring to a boil. Place the egg yolks and sugar in the bowl, and place the bowl on top of the saucepan of boiling water.

Whisk the eggs and sugar over the heat until the mixture starts to thicken and become creamy. Add the warm milk, a little at a time, then the lemon zest.

Keep whisking until the mixture is thick and custard-like. Remove the bowl from the heat and fold in the ground almonds. Put the custard in a clean bowl, cover and place in the fridge. Serve when the custard is cold.

Variations for wellbeing
Gluten intolerance – enjoy as is
Dairy intolerance – use goat's or sheep's milk instead of regular milk
IBS – use lactose-free milk instead of regular milk; small serves only
Lactose intolerance – use lactose-free milk instead of regular milk

Crostoli

These little fried pastries are made of nothing more than dough, and, as a result, they can be quite bland. The sweetness comes from the powdering of sugar at the very end, so don't be afraid to give them a really good dusting. In Italy, these are often eaten at breakfast time, accompanied by a strong coffee. They also make a great afternoon snack. They can be stored for several days in an airtight container.

Makes about 30

3 free-range eggs
3 tablespoons sugar
85 ml (2¾ fl oz) milk
65 ml (2¼ fl oz) cup rum
60 g (2¼ oz) butter, softened
finely grated zest of 1 lemon
a pinch of salt
600 g (1¼ lb) plain flour,
  plus extra for dusting
500 ml (18 fl oz) vegetable oil
icing sugar for dusting

Place the eggs and sugar in a bowl and whisk until you get a thick, frothy mixture. Add the milk, rum, butter, lemon zest and salt.

Sift ¾ of the flour into another bowl. Make a well in the centre and add the egg and sugar mixture; fold gently, using a fork. Add the remaining flour, a little at a time, until the mixture becomes dough-like.

Transfer onto a floured work surface and gently knead the dough until it's smooth and pliable. Divide the dough into about 4 pieces (this makes it easier to handle). Roll the pieces until they are about 3 mm (⅛ in) thick, and then slice into strips 2 cm (¾ in) wide.

Set out a plate lined with a few pieces of kitchen paper. Heat the oil in a heavy-based saucepan. Test the heat by dropping in a pinch of flour: if it starts to sizzle, the oil is ready to fry. Drop the strips of dough into the oil, a few at a time. Cook until golden brown, then drain on kitchen paper. Dust generously with icing sugar.

Variations for wellbeing

Lactose intolerance – enjoy as is

Dairy intolerance – use goat's or sheep's milk instead of regular milk; use dairy-free margarine instead of butter

IBS – suitable only if eaten in small serves

Gluten intolerance – not suitable

andiamo

(let's go)

'I DON'T WANT YOU SITTING AROUND LOOKING LONGINGLY AT PHOTOGRAPHS OF COMPLICATED DISHES THAT YOU COULD NEVER HOPE TO REPLICATE IN YOUR OWN HOME. I WANT YOU IN THE KITCHEN, SLEEVES ROLLED UP, MUSIC ON, GLASS OF WINE IN HAND ... EXPERIENCING FIRST-HAND THE PLEASURE OF GOOD FOOD AND THE PRIVILEGE OF COOKING IT FOR OTHERS.'

Battered and fried apple

I first ate these on the ski slopes of St Moritz, where they are sold in the cafes at the bottom of ski runs. You can pull up on your skis and buy a cardboard cone with about 3 or 4 rings of apple, steaming hot and deliciously sweet. And because you've just flogged yourself on the slopes, you actually feel quite virtuous consuming a few rounds. For a more Australian feel, use pineapple instead of apple. These are a great snack, but can also be served for dessert with a dollop of ice cream.

Serves 4

½ teaspoon dried yeast
1½ teaspoons unsalted butter
2 tablespoons plain flour
65 ml (2¼ fl oz) milk
2 free-range eggs
4 tablespoons castor sugar
4 cooking apples, peeled
2 tablespoons cinnamon
750 ml (1¼ pints) vegetable oil

Dissolve the yeast in a tablespoon of warm water. Melt the butter over a low heat and set aside.

Bring together the flour, milk, eggs, 1½ tablespoons of the sugar, yeast and melted butter in a bowl, and mix the ingredients to form a smooth batter.

Remove the core of each apple using an apple corer or a fine knife, leaving the outside shape of the apple intact. Cut the apples into 1 cm (½ in) slices. Lay the slices on a plate and sprinkle with ½ tablespoon of the sugar.

Set out a plate lined with a few pieces of kitchen paper. On another plate, place the remaining 2 tablespoons of sugar and the cinnamon – use a spoon to combine well.

Heat the oil in a heavy-based saucepan. Test the heat by dropping in a pinch of flour: if it starts to sizzle, the oil is ready to fry.

Working with small batches, dip the apple rings into the batter, then drop them into the oil. Fry until the batter is golden brown all over. Drain on kitchen paper, then toss the battered apples in the cinnamon sugar.

These are best served hot and crunchy.

Variations for wellbeing
Lactose intolerance – enjoy as is
Dairy intolerance – use goat's or sheep's milk instead of regular milk
Gluten intolerance – use maize cornflour instead of plain flour
IBS – not suitable

Crème brûlée

This classic dessert has a number of things going for it: it's easy to make, it tastes great and it looks really fancy. You'll need small ovenproof ramekins – a mini version of those big white soufflé dishes that abound in kitchen shops. Make sure you have a bit of time available: in addition to the cooking time (1 hour), you'll need a couple of hours to rest the custard.

The recipe calls for 8 egg yolks. Rather than get rid of all those eggwhites, whisk them up to make a baking 'case' for a piece of meat or fish; the method is described in Snapper Baked in Eggwhites with Fennel, Mint and Lemon (see page 125).

Serves 6

600 ml (1 pint) pure cream
2 free-range eggs
8 free-range egg yolks
500 g (1 lb) castor sugar
brown sugar for topping

Preheat the oven to 180°C (360°F). Warm the cream in a saucepan. Place the whole eggs, the egg yolks and the sugar in a bowl, and whisk until pale and thick. Continue to whisk as you add the warm cream – very slowly – to the mixture.

Pour or spoon the mixture through a fine sieve (such as a tea strainer) into 6 small ovenproof moulds. Half fill a baking dish with water, and place the moulds in the dish (make sure the water level is not more than halfway up the sides of the moulds). Place in the oven and bake for 1 hour.

Once done, remove the moulds from the baking dish (be careful, as the surrounding water will be very hot). Allow to cool, then cover the moulds with plastic film and chill in the fridge for a couple of hours.

Just before serving, sprinkle the tops with brown sugar. Preheat the griller to its highest setting. Place the moulds under the griller; leave them there just long enough to caramelise the sugar; remove before the custard starts to melt. If you're serious about desserts, you might want to invest in a small blowtorch, which will give you much greater control when caramelising – try your local kitchen shop or hardware store.

Variations for wellbeing

Gluten intolerance – enjoy as is

IBS, lactose intolerance – small serves only

Dairy intolerance – not suitable

Peaches baked with amaretto

The method described here is excellent for peaches that are a little out of season: the biscuits and liquor provide a flavour hit, while the oven-cooking softens the flesh. If the peaches are really ripe, I'll often just grill them plain and serve them with crème fraîche.

Serves 4

butter for greasing
4 large peaches, white or yellow
20 amaretti biscuits, crushed
4 tablespoons amaretto liqueur or rum
100 g (3½ oz) brown sugar

Preheat the oven to 200°C (400°F) and grease a baking tray with a bit of butter.

Wash the peaches in cold water and pat them dry with kitchen paper. Cut them in half and remove the stones. Using a teaspoon, make a little hollow, about 2 cm (¾ in) in diameter, in each half, reserving the scooped-out peach flesh.

Place the crushed biscuits in a bowl, along with the reserved bits of peach flesh, the amaretto liqueur (or rum) and ¾ of the sugar. Mix well. Fill the hollowed peach halves with the biscuit mixture.

Arrange the peaches in a single layer on a baking tray, and sprinkle with the remaining sugar. Bake for about 30 minutes. Serve immediately with a dollop of ice cream.

Variations for wellbeing

Dairy intolerance, lactose intolerance – enjoy as is
Gluten intolerance – use gluten-free amaretti biscuits
IBS – not suitable

Zabaglione Served Chilled

Zabaglione served chilled

Zabaglione is marsala-flavoured custard. The version most people would be familiar with is the one made on the spot and served hot. This version, served frozen, is more like ice cream than custard, and it works well in summer alongside a bit of fresh fruit.

Serves 4–6

6 eggs, separated
100 g (3½ oz) castor sugar
1 glass good-quality marsala or your favourite
  dessert wine
372 ml (13 fl oz) double cream

Choose a largish mixing bowl and a saucepan of approximately the same size – the bowl should be able to sit comfortably on the saucepan. Half fill the saucepan with water and bring to a simmer. Place the egg yolks, sugar and marsala in the bowl, then place the bowl on top of the saucepan of simmering water. Whisk the mixture until it increases in volume and becomes quite thick. Remove the bowl from the heat and allow the mixture to cool.

In a separate bowl, whisk the eggwhites until soft peaks form; in another bowl, whip the cream until it thickens. Add the cream and then the eggwhites to the marsala mix, using a spatula to gently fold the ingredients together; keep a light touch when doing this or you'll knock the air out of the eggwhites. Pour the mixture into a suitably sized mould or dish (high-sided), cover with plastic film and set in the freezer for about 6 hours.

Variations for wellbeing

Gluten intolerance – enjoy as is

Dairy intolerance – use goat's milk crème fraîche instead of cream

Lactose intolerance – suitable only if eaten in small serves

IBS – not suitable

Fresh fig and pecorino seadas

Seadas are little pockets of sweet pasta dough. They probably originated in Sardinia, but the first time I came across them was at the Four Seasons in Milan.

Serves 4

100 g (3½ oz) fresh figs, peeled and diced
50 g (2 oz) good-quality pecorino cheese, finely diced
a good pinch of sugar
1 teaspoon cinnamon
1 quantity Sweet Pasta Dough (see page 191)
500 ml (18 fl oz) vegetable oil
honey for drizzling
icing sugar for dusting

Place the figs, pecorino, sugar and cinnamon in a bowl, and mix well.

To make the pastry cases, roll the sweet pasta dough by hand (see page 192). Alternatively, use a pasta machine: feed each sheet through the rollers a couple of times, gradually decreasing the thickness setting, in order to get a smooth effect.

Cut the sheet/s of pasta into 5 cm (2 in) squares. On each square, place a teaspoon of the fig mixture. Brush the edges with a little water. Fold the dough to make a triangle.

Heat the oil in a heavy-based saucepan. Test the heat by dropping in a pinch of flour: if it starts to sizzle, the oil is ready to fry. Working with small batches, fry the seadas until they are golden brown. Drain on kitchen paper, then serve immediately, with a drizzle of honey and a dusting of icing sugar.

Variations for wellbeing

Lactose intolerance – enjoy as is

Dairy intolerance – use goat's or sheep's cheese instead of pecorino

Gluten intolerance, IBS – not suitable

Cherry pie

Cherry pie is not, of course, particularly Italian. I included this recipe at the suggestion of my partner, Georgia. She pointed out, quite rightly, that cookbooks these days rarely carry recipes for classic desserts like this, and that while everyone loves a cherry pie, no one knows how to cook one – so here it is! It's worth noting that cherries are expensive, even at the peak of their season. However, a tart like this goes a long way: it will serve at least 10 on the night, and you'll have plenty left over for the lunchbox.

Serves 10–12

800 g (1¾ lb) ripe cherries, stoned
juice of 2 lemons
1 cinnamon stick
150 g (5 oz) sugar
300 g (10 oz) cherry jam
2 tablespoons kirsch
150 g (5 oz) butter, plus extra for greasing
1 quantity Sweet Pastry (see page 195)

Preheat the oven to 190°C (375°F).

Place the cherries in a bowl with the lemon juice, cinnamon stick and sugar; give the bowl a bit of a shake to combine the ingredients.

In a small saucepan, combine the jam, kirsch and butter. Simmer gently for 5 minutes, then set aside.

Butter a 30 cm (12 in) loose-bottomed flan tin. Coarsely grate about ¾ of the pastry into the tin, then use your fingertips to press the grated pastry evenly across the base and up the sides.

Using a pastry brush, spread the jam mixture over the pastry base. Drain the cherries of excess water, and scatter across the tart.

Roll the remaining pastry between 2 pieces of plastic film. Cut the pastry into strips long enough and wide enough to form a lattice pattern across the cherries. Using a sharp knife, trim the strips to neaten the edges.

Bake in the oven for about 30 minutes. Serve hot or cold, with ice cream or cream.

Variations for wellbeing
Lactose intolerance – enjoy as is
Dairy intolerance – use dairy-free margarine instead of butter
Gluten intolerance, IBS – not suitable

Kirsch.

Panettone

The panettone you'll find in Italian delis has a sponge-like texture. This version is a little denser and heavier, more like your regular fruitcake. It's lightly spiced and wonderfully sweet. You can use this cake to make a really rich and impressive dessert. Cool the cake after baking and cut off its bottom. Scoop out the inside, leaving the shell intact. Combine the scooped-out cake with a generous cupful of coffee ice cream, and stir well. Put the mixture inside the cake shell, then replace the cake's bottom, before placing the cake, topside up, on a platter. Serve immediately – with a health warning!

Serves 8

**110 g (4 oz) unsalted butter,
  plus extra for greasing
2 free-range eggs
225 g (8 oz) castor sugar
1 teaspoon finely grated lemon zest
1 teaspoon finely grated orange zest
1 teaspoon vanilla extract
500 g (1 lb) plain (all-purpose) flour
2 teaspoons baking powder
2 teaspoons fine-grained salt
250 ml (9 fl oz) buttermilk
250 g (9 oz) slivered almonds
350 g (12 oz) sultanas
400 g (14 oz) mixed dried fruits,
  roughly chopped
icing sugar for dusting**

Preheat the oven to 160°C (320°F). Butter a 20 cm (8 in) springform cake tin, and line with lightly buttered baking paper.

Melt the butter in a small saucepan, and set aside to cool. In a large bowl, combine the eggs and castor sugar, and beat until thick and pale. Beat in the cooled butter, along with the lemon and orange zest, and the vanilla.

In a separate bowl, combine the flour, baking powder and salt. Fold this mixture into the egg and sugar mixture, then beat in the buttermilk. Stir in the almonds, sultanas and mixed dried fruit.

Pour the mixture into the lined cake tin. Bake for about 90 minutes. If the top starts to brown and the centre is not cooked, cover loosely with aluminium foil. To test if the cake is done, insert a skewer – it should come out clean.

Cool the panettone, then dust with icing sugar.

Variations for wellbeing
Dairy intolerance – use goat's or sheep's milk instead of regular milk; use dairy-free margarine instead of butter
Lactose intolerance – use lactose-free milk instead of regular milk
Gluten intolerance, IBS – not suitable

Bomboloni – Italian doughnuts

Bomboloni are sold all over Italy, often from vans parked on the roadside. The doughnuts here are finished with a light dusting of sugar, but you can use cinnamon sugar, and if you have a piping bag, you can go over the top with fillings such as jam, custard crème and chocolate crème. A word of warning: you'll need to set aside 5 hours for the dough to rest, then 1 hour for it to rise.

30 g (1 oz) dried yeast
250 ml (9 fl oz) milk
800 g (1¾ lb) plain flour,
    plus extra for dusting
4 tablespoons sugar
2 free-range eggs
25 g (1 oz) butter, softened
1 teaspoon finely grated orange zest
a pinch of salt
1 tablespoon castor sugar
500 ml (18 fl oz) vegetable oil

Place the yeast and milk in a small bowl and use a fork to stir well. In a large bowl combine the flour, sugar, eggs, butter, orange zest and salt. Add the milk and yeast. Using your hands, work the ingredients until you have a smooth dough. Place the dough in a bowl and cover with plastic film. Rest the dough in the fridge for about 5 hours.

Take the dough from the fridge and place it on a clean floured surface. Roll the dough to a thickness of 2 cm (¾ in); dust with flour to prevent sticking. Using a biscuit cutter or glass, cut the dough into disks.

Line a tray with greaseproof paper and place the disks on the paper – leave some space between the disks to allow the dough to rise. Cover loosely with plastic film, then put the tray in a warm place for 40–60 minutes.

Set out a plate of castor sugar. Line another plate with a few pieces of kitchen paper. Heat the oil in a heavy-based saucepan. Test the heat by dropping in a pinch of flour: if it starts to sizzle, the oil is ready to fry. Fry the disks of dough a few at a time. When they are golden brown on both sides, remove from the oil. Drain the doughnuts on kitchen paper, then toss them in the sugar.

Serve hot or keep for later.

Variations for wellbeing

Dairy intolerance – use goat's or sheep's milk instead of regular milk; use dairy-free margarine instead of butter

Lactose intolerance – use lactose-free milk instead of regular milk

Gluten intolerance, IBS – not suitable

Chocolate and olive oil tart

This recipe uses couverture chocolate, a high-quality chocolate with a rich, complex flavour and glossy texture; look for it in specialty food stores. The other key ingredient is olive oil. Avoid the big peppery or grassy olive oils, and go for something light and a bit fruity. Plenty of stores and markets now offer olive oil tastings.

butter for greasing
1 quantity Sweet Pastry (see page 195)
dried chickpeas, lentils or rice for baking blind
300 g (10 oz) dark couverture chocolate, chopped
5 tablespoons double cream
5 tablespoons extra-virgin olive oil
4 free-range eggs
100 g (3½ oz) castor (superfine) sugar
1 tablespoon maple syrup

Choose a loose-bottomed flan tin, 24 cm (9½ in) in diameter and 3 cm (1¼ in) high, or as close to this size as possible. Butter lightly. Using a cheese grater, grate the pastry into the tin, then, using your fingertips, press the pastry across the base and up the sides. Put the pastry case into the fridge for 30 minutes.

Preheat the oven to 180°C (360°F). Remove the pastry case from the fridge and line it with baking paper or foil, then scatter with a couple of handfuls of chickpeas, lentils or rice, or other similar dried ingredient. The pastry should have enough weight on it to prevent it bubbling as it cooks. Baking a tart like this – without a filling – is known as baking blind. Place the pastry case in the oven and bake for 20 minutes; once done, allow it to cool in the tin. Reduce the oven heat to 150°C (300°F).

Choose a bowl that will sit comfortably on top of a medium-sized saucepan. Half fill the saucepan with water and bring to a simmer. Place the chocolate, cream and olive oil in the bowl, and place the bowl on top of the saucepan. Stir to combine; once the chocolate has melted, remove the bowl from the heat and set aside.

In a separate bowl, whisk the eggs, sugar and maple syrup until thick and pale; using a spatula, fold the chocolate mixture into the egg mixture.

Pour the filling into the pastry shell. Bake in the oven for 40 minutes or until the chocolate has set. Serve cold, with crème fraîche or double cream.

Variations for wellbeing
Lactose intolerance – enjoy as is
Dairy intolerance – use goat's milk crème fraîche instead of cream; use dairy-free margarine instead of butter
Gluten intolerance, IBS – not suitable

I love
chocolate
tart !

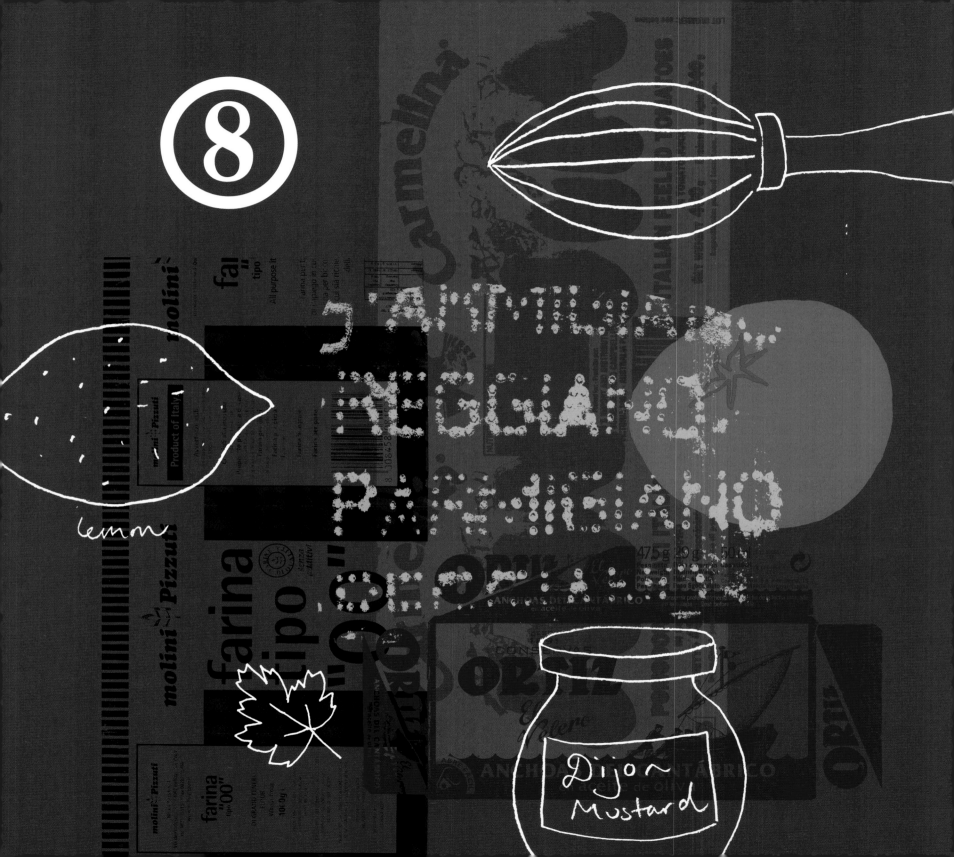

BASES AND BASICS

eggs

Breadcrumbs

There's no excuse for buying packet crumbs when you can make a far superior version by rounding up the leftovers from the bottom of your breadbin.

Makes about 250 g

1 small loaf ciabatta bread
1 tablespoon rosemary leaves,
finely chopped
1 teaspoon dried chilli
(optional)
3 tablespoons olive oil
sea salt
freshly ground black pepper

Preheat the oven to 220°C (430°F). Use your hands to break the ciabatta into 5 cm (2 in) pieces. Place the bread onto a baking tray (you may need a second tray). Scatter with rosemary and dried chilli (if using). Drizzle with olive oil and season with salt and pepper. Bake in the oven until the bread turns a rich golden colour. Shake the tray from time to time so the bread cooks evenly.

After the bread has cooled, place it in a food processor and pulse it to the consistency of coarse sand. You can also crumb the bread by rubbing it between the palms of your hands.

Variations for wellbeing
Dairy intolerance, lactose intolerance – enjoy as is
Gluten intolerance, IBS – use gluten-free bread

Green vegetables, braised

This is a one-size-fits-all recipe for the cooking of green vegetables. It's what you serve whenever you need a tasty, healthy side dish.

Serves 2

green vegetables (enough for 2)
2 tablespoons extra-virgin olive oil
1 clove garlic, chopped
2 anchovy fillets (optional)
a pinch of dried chilli
¼ glass white wine
finely grated zest and juice
of 1 lemon
sea salt
freshly ground black pepper

Bring a saucepan of salted water to a boil. Trim your greens as appropriate. Plunge them into the boiling water and cook for a couple of minutes, or until they are just starting to soften. Refresh under cold running water, then drain on kitchen paper.

Heat the oil in a frying pan. Over a low-to-medium heat, sauté the garlic, anchovies (if using) and dried chilli for 5 minutes – don't let the garlic start to colour. Raise the heat and add the greens. Cook for a couple of minutes. Splash in the wine and let it evaporate. Add the lemon juice and zest, and season with salt and pepper. Serve immediately.

Variations for wellbeing
Dairy intolerance, gluten intolerance, lactose intolerance – enjoy as is
IBS – do not use asparagus, artichokes, green beans, onions, leek or chicory

Eggwhite batter

This is a very light batter. I love it because it doesn't leave you feeling like you have eaten a cup of flour, which can be the effect of heavier batters. An important

tip is to use a spatula or wooden spoon to fold the batter into the eggwhites, and to do it very gently. That way, you won't knock the air out of the whites.

150 g (5 oz) plain
flour
a pinch of salt
2 free-range eggwhites

Place the flour and salt in a bowl. Add about 1 cup of warm water. Whisk the ingredients together to form a smooth, thick batter, then pour through a fine strainer into a clean bowl. Cover with plastic film and place in the fridge. Remove after an hour or so. In a separate bowl, whisk the eggwhites until soft peaks form. Very gently, fold the eggwhites into the batter.

Variations for wellbeing
Dairy intolerance, lactose intolerance – enjoy as is
Gluten intolerance, IBS – use 70 g (2½ oz) each of rice flour and maize cornflour instead of plain flour

Mayonnaise

This versatile condiment can be flavoured in any number of ways – see Variations, opposite.

2 free-range egg yolks
1 teaspoon dijon mustard
about 300 ml (10 fl oz) olive oil
juice of ½ lemon
sea salt
freshly ground black pepper

Put the yolks and mustard into a mixing bowl and whisk well. Very slowly, drizzle

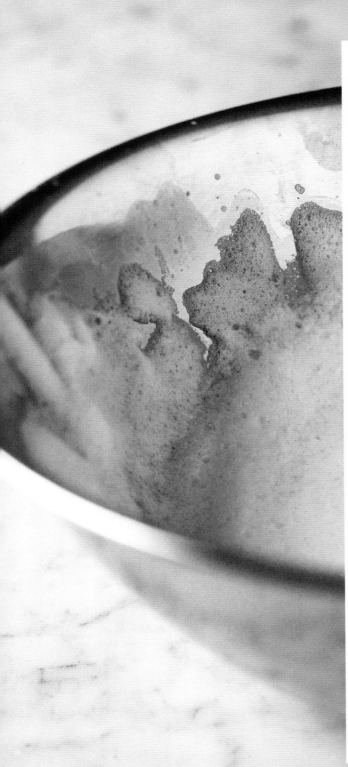

in a small amount of oil. Whisk until the yolks have absorbed the oil. Continue to add the oil, a little at a time, whisking every time. You are aiming for a fairly thick substance that has a glossy, pale-yellow finish. When the mayonnaise is about the right consistency, squeeze in a little lemon juice and season with salt and pepper.

Variations for wellbeing

Dairy intolerance, gluten intolerance, IBS, lactose intolerance – enjoy as is (this also applies to Variations below)

Variations – aïoli, saffron mayonnaise, herb mayonnaise

Mayonnaise can be flavoured in a variety of ways. Aïoli is a strongly flavoured garlic mayonnaise, common in Spain and southern France. To make, crush garlic in a mortar (about 3–4 cloves). Combine with egg yolks, then add the oil as you would with normal mayonnaise. For a saffron flavour, infuse 2–3 strands of saffron in a really small amount of warm water, then whisk the saffron-infused water into the finished mayonnaise. For herb infusions, grind a variety of herbs in a mortar until paste-like (you may need a dab of oil), then whisk into the finished mayonnaise.

Pasta dough

There are many different types of pasta dough, using various combinations of flour and flavourings, but there are only two definitive rules for pasta-making: one, keep your workbench clean, dry and well floured; two, enjoy it.

Basic pasta dough

500 g (1 lb) white pasta flour or
**   plain wholemeal flour**
a pinch of salt
4 free-range eggs

Sift the flour and salt onto a clean bench. Make a hollow in the flour. Crack the eggs into the hollow, then use a fork to gradually work in the eggs. Be careful not to break the wall of flour or the eggs will run out. Once the ingredients have combined, knead the dough (see following page).

Variations for wellbeing

Dairy intolerance, lactose intolerance – enjoy as is
Gluten intolerance, IBS – use Gluten-free Pasta Dough (see following page)

Sweet pasta dough

The Italians use sweet pasta dough for making fried desserts such as seadas. Use exactly the same recipe as for Basic Pasta Dough (see above). Use white flour, not wholemeal, and replace the salt with a generous pinch of sugar and a little ground cinnamon. You may even want to add a few drops of alcohol, such as amaretto.

Variations for wellbeing

Dairy intolerance, lactose intolerance – enjoy as is
Gluten intolerance, IBS – use Gluten-free Pasta Dough (see following page)

Buckwheat-flour pasta dough

Despite its name, buckwheat is not wheat but a type of herb. It's not all that common, but you will find it in health-food stores and other specialty food shops.

200 g (7 oz) buckwheat flour
100 g (3½ oz) pasta flour
a pinch of salt
1 free-range egg
3 tablespoons milk

Sift the 2 sorts of flour into a bowl, then add the salt, egg and milk, along with 3 tablespoons of water; using your hands, fold the ingredients to combine.

Variations for wellbeing

Lactose intolerance – enjoy as is

Dairy intolerance – use goat's or sheep's milk
    instead of regular milk

Gluten intolerance, IBS – not suitable; use
    Gluten-free Pasta Dough (see below)

Gluten-free pasta dough

This recipe calls for a few ingredients that may seem a bit exotic. The different types of flour can be sourced from health-food shops and some supermarkets. Rice flour can be found in Asian grocery stores. Xanthan gum is an emulsifier made from fermented corn syrup. It, too, can be found in health-food shops and some supermarkets.

85 g (3 oz) tapioca flour
    or potato flour
85 g (3 oz) fine rice flour
    or maize cornflour
¾ teaspoon salt
1 teaspoon xanthan gum
2 free-range eggs
1 teaspoon extra-virgin
    olive oil

Combine the flours, salt and xantham gum in a mixing bowl, and make a well in the centre using your hands. Add the eggs and extra-virgin olive oil to the flour; use a fork to mix the ingredients until they form a dough.

Variations for wellbeing

Dairy intolerance, gluten intolerance, IBS,
    lactose intolerance – enjoy as is

Kneading and rolling pasta dough

Scatter some flour onto a clean, dry surface. Place the dough on the surface, and start to knead. Use the heels of your hands to push the dough downwards and then forwards. Fold the dough in half, turn it a little, and continue to knead. Keep going until the dough is smooth and elastic – this should take about 10 minutes. If the dough is sticky, add more flour. Place the dough in a bowl, cover it with plastic film and allow it to rest for 30 minutes before rolling.

Re-flour your work surface. Use your hands to flatten the pasta dough as much as possible. Roll the dough from the centre, using a rolling pin; if the dough starts to stick, dust it with flour (use maize cornflour if intolerant).

Once the dough is about 5 mm (¼ in) thick, turn it over to prevent moisture gathering on the underside. To do this, curl the far edge of the dough over the rolling pin, then gently roll the pin towards you. Unroll the dough on its reverse side, and dust with more flour. Keep rolling the dough until it's no thicker than fine cardboard.

Polenta

Polenta is easy and versatile. Serve it hot alongside a nice winter stew, or allow it to cool, then cut it into slices, and grill.

Serves 4–6

250 g (9 oz) polenta
100 g (3½ oz) butter
a handful of freshly grated
 parmesan cheese
sea salt
freshly ground black pepper

Put 750 ml (1¼ pints) of water into a saucepan and bring to a boil. Gradually add the polenta, stirring with a wooden spoon. As the polenta thickens, stir quite vigorously to prevent lumps forming.

When all the polenta has been added, reduce the heat to a light simmer; cook for about 40 minutes, stirring continually. Once the polenta has begun to pull away from the bottom of the pot, stir in the butter and the parmesan, and season well with salt and pepper. Serve immediately.

Variations for wellbeing

Gluten intolerance, IBS, lactose intolerance,
 – enjoy as is
Dairy intolerance – omit parmesan; use
 dairy-free margarine instead of butter

Olive oil

In my pantry, I have different grades of olive oil, as well as vegetable oil, which I use for some kinds of deep-frying. I always have a top-quality extra-virgin olive oil on hand. Extra-virgin olive oil is made from choice olives, which are crushed soon after harvest. To be graded extra-virgin, the oil needs to have an acidity level no higher than 1 per cent. Because much of the flavour of extra-virgin olive oil is lost when heated, I reserve my best oil (the expensive stuff) for use in the preparation of raw foods, such as salads and carpaccio, and for finishing pasta, stews, grilled meat, fish – really, any dish that benefits from a good drizzle, post-cooking. There are great-quality oils from all over the globe, and they vary in flavour and colour. Specialist food stores offer oil tastings from time to time, and certainly the staff at such places should be able to point you in the direction of an oil that will suit the food you like to cook.

I also keep a lesser quality, less-expensive extra-virgin olive oil on hand, which I use for cooking – frying meat and vegetables, adding oil to pasta water. You can often buy this kind of oil in bulk (4-litre tins). Alternatively, you can use a straight olive oil for cooking. This kind of oil is generally blended; it has a higher acidity and the flavour is less fruity.

If you buy oil in bulk, decant it into bottles, and store the bottles in a cool, dark place.

Variations for wellbeing

Dairy intolerance, gluten intolerance, IBS,
 lactose intolerance – enjoy as is

Parmesan cheese

When shopping for parmesan, buy parmigiano reggiano or grana padano. These cheeses are both made using traditional methods, although with parmigiano reggiano, the methods are more complex and the ageing period is longer – 24 months compared to around 15 months. It is considered a better cheese and is certainly more expensive. For that reason, use it to finish dishes (to grate or shave over cooked pasta or salads), or simply on its own as part of a selection of antipasto, rather than in cooked dishes, such as risotto.

Buy parmesan in small wedges. Don't store it in plastic film, as the cheese will sweat. I wrap mine in greaseproof paper, but traditionalists would argue for the use of a damp cloth. Only grate the parmesan as you need it.

Variations for wellbeing

Gluten intolerance, IBS, lactose intolerance
 – enjoy as is
Dairy intolerance – not suitable

Salsa dragoncella

Salsa dragoncella is great with roasted or boiled meats. It will keep for several days in the fridge.

Makes about 60 g

a small handful of flat-leaf
 parsley
a small handful of tarragon
2 cloves garlic, peeled
2 tablespoons Breadcrumbs
 (see page 190)
5 tablespoons extra-virgin
 olive oil
sea salt
freshly ground black pepper

Chop the herbs and garlic very finely.
Place them in a bowl with the breadcrumbs.
Gradually add the oil, mixing well. Season
with salt and pepper.

Variations for wellbeing
Dairy intolerance, lactose intolerance – enjoy as is
Gluten intolerance, IBS – use gluten-free
   breadcrumbs

Salsa verde

There are many versions of salsa verde
(green sauce). Some recipes add bread,
others use pine nuts. Some people use
a food processor to chop the herbs, but
I do it by hand to get a nice rough texture.
Salsa verde goes well with meat, poultry
and fish.

Makes about 75 g

2 cloves garlic, finely chopped
3–6 anchovies
1 tablespoon salted capers,
   roughly chopped
a small handful of flat-leaf
   parsley, chopped
a small handful of basil leaves,
   finely torn
5 mint leaves, sliced
finely grated zest and juice
   of 1 lemon
extra-virgin olive oil
sea salt
freshly ground black pepper

In a mortar, pound the garlic and anchovies.
Add the chopped capers, herbs and lemon
zest and juice. Drizzle in enough olive oil to
just cover the herbs. Season with salt and
pepper; mix a little before serving.

Variations for wellbeing
Dairy intolerance, gluten intolerance, IBS,
   lactose intolerance – enjoy as

Sterilising jars

Bring a large saucepan of water to a boil.
Place the jars in the water so the jars are
fully submerged. Remove after about
5 minutes. Drain the jars upside down
on kitchen paper until they are completely
dry. Use as soon as possible.

Stocks

The quality of the stock you use really
influences the overall flavour of a dish,
so use good-quality ingredients.

Variations for wellbeing
Gluten intolerance, lactose intolerance –
   enjoy all stock recipes as written
Dairy intolerance – use dairy-free margarine
   instead of butter (Fish Stock)
IBS – omit onion and double the amount
   of celery (all stock recipes)

Beef stock

Makes 4 litres

1 kg (2 lb 4 oz) beef bones
1 large carrot, roughly chopped
2 onions, roughly chopped
3 sticks celery, roughly chopped
3 bay leaves
½ bunch parsley stalks,
   roughly chopped
1 leek, roughly chopped
3 tomatoes, roughly chopped

To make dark stock, roast the bones in the
oven for about 1 hour before placing them
in the stockpot.

Place all the ingredients into a large
saucepan or stockpot and cover with
cold water. Bring the water to a very
gentle simmer, and cook for 2–4 hours
(the longer you cook, the more intense the
flavour). Every so often, remove the scum
that rises to the surface, using a sieve.
When the stock is done, strain it into
a container, and refrigerate or freeze.

Chicken stock

Make an instant and delicious soup using
this stock recipe: to the hot stock add
4 eggs, beaten, and a handful each of
chopped parsley and parmesan; whisk
for 30 seconds, then serve.

Makes 2 litres

1 free-range chicken,
   about 2 kg (4 lb 8 oz)
2 sticks celery, roughly chopped
2 medium carrots, roughly chopped
2 onions, roughly chopped
4 black peppercorns

Place all the ingredients in a large saucepan
or stockpot and cover with cold water. Cook
at a low simmer. Every so often, remove
the scum that rises to the surface, using
a sieve. After about 3 hours, strain the
stock into a container, and refrigerate or
freeze. Discard the vegetables, but keep
the chicken for use in soups or pasta sauces
and fillings.

Fish stock

Makes 1.5 litres

100 g (3½ oz) butter
**600 g (1¼ lb) fish bones or whole
    fish, rinsed under cold water
    and roughly chopped**
2 sticks celery, roughly chopped
2 onions, roughly chopped
2 bay leaves
**1 bunch parsley stalks,
    roughly chopped**

Melt the butter in a large saucepan or
stockpot over a medium heat; add all
ingredients and sauté gently. Once the
bones start to colour, add 2 litres
of cold water; bring to a simmer, and cook
for 40 minutes, skimming the scum or
foam that rises to the surface, using a
sieve. Drain the liquid into a
container and discard the bones;
refrigerate or freeze.

Vegetable stock

Makes 1.5 litres

4 tablespoons olive oil
2 onions, roughly chopped
2 carrots, roughly chopped
2 sticks celery, roughly chopped
**2 leeks (white part only),
    roughly chopped**
2 cloves garlic, peeled
**1 bunch parsley stalks,
    roughly chopped**
8 black peppercorns
2 bay leaves

Heat the olive oil in a large saucepan
or stockpot over a medium heat; add
all ingredients and gently sauté for about
10 minutes. Add 2 litres of cold water;
simmer for 1 hour, skimming the scum or
foam that rises to the surface, using a
sieve. Once the stock is ready, discard the
vegetables and strain the liquid into a
container; refrigerate or freeze.

Sweet pastry

Makes enough for 2 small flan tins

**300 g (10 oz) plain
    flour, sifted**
**200 g (7 oz) unsalted butter,
    cubed and softened**
3 large free-range egg yolks
60 g (2 oz) castor sugar
a pinch of salt

If you have a food processor, pulse the
flour and butter until the mixture resembles
coarse breadcrumbs. Alternatively, use your
hands to get the same effect.

Add the egg yolks and sugar. Process or mix
the ingredients until they combine to form
a smooth ball of pastry.

Divide the pastry into 2 balls and wrap each
ball in plastic film. Place pastry balls in the
fridge for at least 1 hour before using.

Variations for wellbeing

Lactose intolerance – enjoy as is
Dairy intolerance – use dairy-free margarine
    instead of butter
Gluten intolerance, IBS – use 150 g (5 oz) rice
    flour, 100 g (3½ oz) cornflour and 50 g
    (2 oz) soy flour, instead of plain flour

THANKS

There are really too many people to thank, but I'm going to give it a go.

Special thanks to Mum and Dad for everything, in particular, for suggesting a career working with knives; to the beautiful Georgia for always being there for me, listening to my wild ideas; to my sister, Lucy, and Jan, Tom and Mary, for their loving support over the years; to Jan Willingham and Jim Irwin for letting me grow up in their restaurants.

A really massive thank you to Jum for being an inspiration and an amazing friend from the moment we met out the back of the River Cafe. Also hugs and kisses to all the Oliver girls, especially Daisy.

To Adam 'Hooften' Garrisson, thank you for your belief in me and your hard work in helping Fifteen Melbourne become a reality. And to Mark Gonzales for making a childhood dream come true by doing a graphic for my 'pro model'.

Big thanks to friends Matt Skinner, Randy, Callan Gorat and Tim Fox for being themselves since those early skateboarding days in suburban car parks.

Thank you to mentor Maurizio Terzini, who, with the gift of an amazing book when I was eighteen, helped me realise the beauty and pleasure of great food.

A colossal thanks to all the chefs I have worked with in Australia, Italy, Switzerland and London, in particular, Rose Gray and Ruth Rogers – extraordinary inspirations – and Pierre-Paolo Caprioglio, who refused to speak to me in English, forcing me to learn Italian in record time, likewise Peter Hall, Maurice Manno, Mauro Marcucci, Paolo, Cordell Khoury, Gennaro Contaldo and Carlo Sciarpa.

Numerous people put a huge effort into this book. Thank you to the talented Sue Shepherd, who turned this publication into something rare: a mainstream cookbook that can be used by people with food intolerances.

A big thanks to designer Danie Pout for giving this book its amazing look, and photographer Mark Chew and assistant Tony Mott for putting up with me during the shoots and, more importantly, producing such great photos. And to the Penguin crew: publisher Julie Gibbs, editor Ingrid Ohlsson, and designers Adam Laszczuk and Deb Brash.

Just a couple more and then I'm done: many thanks to Lisa Sullivan and all the lovely people at Fresh Partners; Damien Pike at Prahran Market for all the chats we've had about your beautiful produce; and the entire Katz/Lovett family.

Index

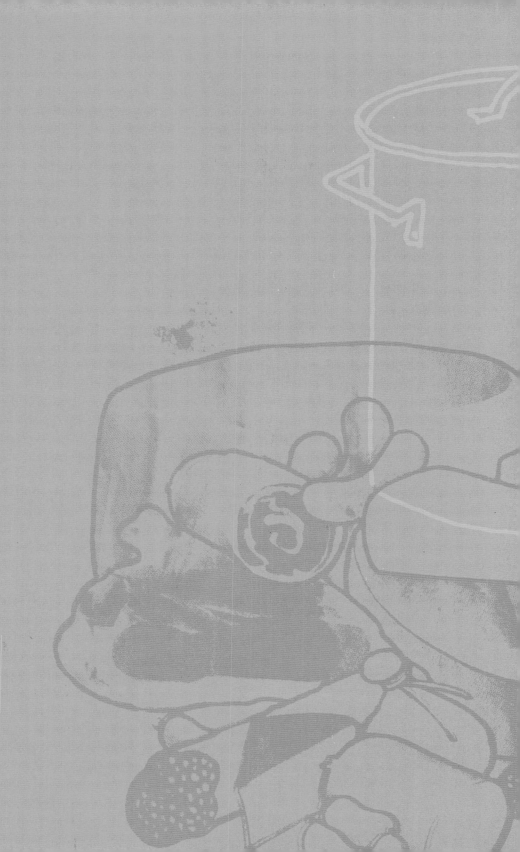

First published 2006
under the title *Daily Italian*
by the Penguin Group (Australia)

Text copyright © Tobie Puttock 2006
Photographs copyright © Mark Chew 2006

First published in the UK in 2007 by Mitchell Beazley,
an imprint of Octopus Publishing Group Limited,
2-4 Heron Quays, London E14 4JP

Design and illustrations by Danie Pout Design
Design assistant Adam Laszczuk
Cover and internal photography by Mark Chew
Additional styling by Michelle Cammiade
Photograph in 'Foreword' by David Loftus
Typeset in ITC Franklin Gothic 11.5/15 pt by
Post Pre-press Group, Brisbane, Queensland
Colour reproduction by Splitting Image, Clayton, Victoria

ISBN13: 978 1 84533 310 2

ISBN10: 1 84533 301 1

A CIP record for this book is available from the British Library.

Printed and bound in China